maximize

maximize

HOW TO DEVELOP EXTRAVAGANT GIVERS
IN YOUR CHURCH

nelson searcy

WITH JENNIFER DYKES HENSON

BakerBooks

a division of Baker Publishing Group
Grand Rapids, Michigan

© 2010 by Nelson Searcy

Published by Baker Books
a division of Baker Publishing Group
P.O. Box 6287, Grand Rapids, MI 49516-6287
www.bakerbooks.com

Printed in the United States of America

Library of Congress Cataloging-in-Publication Data
Searcy, Nelson.
    Maximize : how to develop extravagant givers in your church / Nelson
Searcy with Jennifer Dykes Henson.
      p. cm.
    Includes bibliographical references.
    ISBN 978-0-8010-7218-5 (pbk.)
    1. Christian giving. I. Henson, Jennifer Dykes. II. Title.
BV772.S43 2010
254′.8—dc22
                                              2010014151

10   11   12   13   14   15   16   7   6   5   4   3   2   1

To my dad and mom, Alton and Patricia Searcy

contents

Acknowledgments   9
Preface   13
Introduction   15

Part 1   Stewardship: Becoming a Fully Developing Follower of Jesus

1. Shining the Light: Illuminating a Taboo Subject   25
2. The Heart of Stewardship: Introducing the Maximize System   37
3. Creating a Culture of Generosity: "Give, and You Will Receive"   49

Part 2   Initial Givers: Raising Up New Givers

4. Cultivating First-Time Gifts: Practical Ways to Help People Cross the Threshold   61

7

5. Easy Does It: Eliminating Unnecessary Barriers to Giving 75
6. Revolutionary Gratitude: A Little Thanks Goes a Long Way 89

Part 3 Systematic Givers: Teaching People to Give When They Are Paid

7. Options Are Not Optional: Providing Various Ways for People to Give 105
8. From First-Time Givers to Regular Givers: Helping People Take the Step 125
9. Money Matters: Financial Management and Quarterly Giving Statements 147

Part 4 Tithers: Challenging People to Become Proportional Givers

10. The Full Tithe: Obedience-Level Giving 167
11. The Giving Challenge: A Revolutionary Tool 181

Part 5 Extravagant Givers: Spurring People to Live like Jesus

12. Extravagant Giving: Learning to Live like Jesus 201
13. Getting Started: First Steps toward Becoming a Fully Resourced Church 217

Afterword 225
Notes 227

acknowledgments

My journey to become a fully developing steward is certainly ongoing, and many people have greatly influenced me along the way. This book is one expression of my journey so far. My eternal gratitude to Jesus Christ for calling me to salvation and later to ministry. While dozens, if not hundreds, of pastors have influenced my thinking on stewardship, two stand above the rest: Ralph Carpenter and Steve Stroope.

Shortly after entering ministry in 1990, I met Preacher Carpenter. He has since gone on to his reward, yet I am grateful for the dozens of hours he invested in me by the fireplace of his book-filled home in North Carolina. I don't think anyone loved preaching on stewardship more than he did. Thank you for igniting that passion in me.

On my way to start The Journey in New York City in 2001, I met Steve Stroope, senior pastor of Lakepointe Church in Rockwall, Texas. No one has impacted my understanding of local church stewardship and local church leadership more

9

than Steve. From our monthly phone calls to his ready wisdom, he has gently guided me to lead a "maximized" church for the glory of God. Steve, I hope you will continue to take my calls for a long time!

In addition, I would like to thank the following pastors and church leaders for influencing my views and shaping my thoughts on stewardship: Randy Alcorn, Elmer Towns, Dave Ramsey, Rick Warren, B. H. Carroll, John Maxwell, Randy Pope, Larry Burkett, and Steve Merrimen of Clergy Advantage. If the theology and applications in this book are correct, you can thank the pastors listed above. If there are mistakes, they are solely mine.

I must also express a huge thanks to my colleagues at The Journey Church, both past and present staff members. Since 2001 I have had the privilege of being the dumbest person on an extremely smart team. Kerrick Thomas and Jason Hatley have especially shaped the thoughts in this book. To the current staff, I love doing church with you! To those God will call to our staff in the future, I'm waiting to hear from you!

My sincere appreciation goes to the team that makes Church Leader Insights happen every day and every week. You have no idea of the impact you are having on pastors around the world. Thank you, Scott Whitaker, Tommy Duke, Cristina Fowler, and Jimmy Britt!

I must also express my thanks to the more than six hundred pastors who have completed one of my Senior Pastors Coaching Networks. Many of the ideas shared in this book were first beta tested on you. Your feedback, improvements, and insights have made this a much stronger book. Thank you for living out the learn-and-return principle. A special thanks to those alumni who shared their testimonies in this book.

Jennifer Dykes Henson has been a partner on my last five books, and to my ongoing amazement she continues to reach new levels with each book. Her skills as a writer, editor, and interpreter are difficult to overstate. I cannot say thank you enough! And I must confess that Jon, Liz, and Pastor Tim (characters you will encounter in the following pages) would not exist without Jen's creative mind. As members at The Journey, Jennifer and her husband, Brian, serve as models of all I discuss in this book.

This is my second book with the tremendously dedicated people at Baker. My thanks to Chad Allen, Jack Kuhatschek, Rod Jantzen, and all the fine folks at Baker Publishing who have made this book infinitely stronger than it was when I submitted the original manuscript.

Finally, I must thank the love of my life, Kelley, and my young son, Alexander. Kelley and I celebrated fifteen years of marriage while I was completing this book. Kelley, I love you now more than ever! Alexander, who will turn four years old just prior to the release of this book, is just now learning that there is something strange and powerful about coins and bills. May God give us the grace to teach him godly habits of stewardship as he continues to grow and mature. Alexander, I love you to the moon and back. Thank you both for your commitment to this book and your continual support.

Jennifer Dykes Henson: thanks, Nelson, for the vision, passion, and integrity you bring to all you do. I am beyond honored to be authoring eternity-changing books with you.

Thanks also to my husband, Brian, for your faith, strength, humor, and love. I thank God every day for you, for the life and dreams he has given us, and for the privilege of pursuing those dreams hand in hand with my best friend.

preface

Imagine you are sitting in your office. (Maybe you actually are!) You hear a rapping on the door and look up to see one of your staff members.

"Hey," you say. "What's going on?"

"I just wanted to talk to you about something. I've had this idea on my mind for a few months now. I really feel like God is leading us to make some changes to the volunteer ministry. We need to be doing more to encourage people to get involved. So I've been thinking that if we could spend a little money on . . ."

Pause.

How do you feel at this moment? When you see the need to use financial resources to take an area of your ministry to the next level, what is your first thought? Is your immediate question a reflective, "Does God want us to do this?" Or is it a reflexive, "Can we afford this?" Are you in a position to operate your church at full throttle, passionately pursuing

God's complete vision, or are you restrained by a budget that always seems to be lacking?

If you are like most church leaders across America, your hands are bound by money-colored handcuffs. You can't tap into God's best design for your church because you are constantly struggling just to cover the basics of your weekly operation. That's where this book comes in. My dream for you is that through these pages you will learn how to unleash the abundant resources God intends for you to have available for his work. In other words, the goal of this book, and the Maximize system contained within, is to help you develop a fully resourced church—one in which you are consistently leading people into biblical stewardship and are free to cooperate with the big plans God has for your future. Are you ready?

introduction

What would your church look like if everyone tithed? Your budget would probably be five times what it is now, since the average churchgoer gave only 2.56 percent of his income last year.[1] What would you do with that kind of budget? Is that too much to imagine? Okay, back it down. What if your budget were just double what it is right now? How many more people would you be able to reach for Jesus? What ministries and opportunities would you be able to engage in that you currently have to say no to? How would a maximized budget affect your missions giving, your church-planting efforts, your evangelistic aggressiveness, and the overall spiritual health of your congregation?

I have a great truth to share with you: God wants your church to have all the money it needs to do the work he calls it to do. In other words, he wants your church to be fully resourced, from within. And he set up a plan for making that happen—a plan that the vast majority of us conveniently ignore. Why would we ignore God's truth on financing the church? Because:

- we are uncomfortable talking about money with our people.
- we came out of a church that never had enough, so we think that's the way it is.
- we aren't following God's best with our own personal finances.
- we don't want to scare off the unchurched by focusing on money too much.
- we believe the myth that there is virtue in being in constant financial need.
- we are used to the status quo of operation.
- we think we should leave the big ministry goals to bigger churches.

Thanks to all these reasons and more, we shy away from God's teaching on stewardship and his plan for a fully resourced church. We allow money, or the lack of it, to create a chasm between the current state of our churches and God's ultimate goal for them. Believe me, I've been there. I understand the hesitancy to step out of the boat. But now I know from personal experience that it is possible to have a budget that allows you to say yes to the ministry opportunities God places in your path. It is possible to have a budget that allows you to operate without the stress of constant lack and that continually helps your people grow in their spiritual lives by teaching them to become biblical stewards of the resources entrusted to them.

Here's my story in brief. (I'll give you much more detail in chapter 2.) Four years into planting The Journey Church in New York City, my staff and I found ourselves face-to-face with the reality that our outside financial sponsorship was going to be wrapping up at the end of the year. We needed a plan to become self-sufficient—quickly. The problem was that we were currently working with a budget of $13,500 per week, and we needed to get that to $18,000 per week be-

How would a maximized budget affect your missions giving, your church-planting efforts, your evangelistic aggressiveness, and the overall spiritual health of your congregation?

fore we could be comfortable with our partners pulling out. You might say we were desperate.

Spurred into action by this desperation, I set out on a journey of study and prayer. I read dozens of books about stewardship. I searched the Bible for God's truth about his people's hearts, money, and the financing of the church. I sought counsel from trusted mentors. I prayed unceasingly for wisdom about godly stewardship in general and our best immediate course of action. Through this process, I developed a step-by-step, biblical, and practical stewardship system to cultivate givers in our church with the short-term goal of increasing our giving by about $5,000 per week. Are you ready to hear what happened? We didn't hit the goal we set; we exceeded it. In six months our giving increased from $13,500 per week to over $22,000 per week. We said good-bye to our outside partners and have been self-sufficient ever since. God is good!

The stewardship system I developed is the same one that still hums beneath the surface of The Journey today, keeping us open and available to passionately pursue God's will. I will dig into every detail of the system—now called Maximize— in the pages ahead. First, I want to be clear: this book is not about tricks or sleight-of-hand ways to get your people to give more. It is about biblical stewardship in our current church culture. My goal is to help you lead your people down the path of discipleship that is found in true stewardship and thereby fully resource your church the way God intends. Through the Maximize system, I have trained hundreds of pastors around the country to raise up new givers and to turn sporadic givers into tithers who ultimately become extravagant givers. The churches I've coached through this system have seen an average 33 percent increase in giving. Many have seen their giving double. You'll meet many of these leaders and hear their stories as this book unfolds.

Here are some questions I'd like you to consider in relation to the church as a whole: Why do we take the offering the way we do? Why is the average pastor untrained to preach on money? What if we preached on money just half as much as Jesus did? Why do we allow people to give their tithes and offerings only on Sunday? What if we provided various ways for people to give? Why has the church adopted its stewardship practices primarily from nonprofit organizations? What if we viewed stewardship as a subset of discipleship, as the Bible teaches?

Most churches never pause long enough to reflect on why things are the way they are. We will ask and answer all these questions and more. I trust that in the pages ahead your stewardship paradigm will shift. Here are just a few examples of what you will discover:

- How to increase your church's giving this Sunday (Yes, this Sunday. There's one mistake most churches make when receiving the offering that can hurt giving by as much as 20 percent.)
- How to encourage every non-giver to give for the first time
- How to turn first-time givers into extravagant givers
- How to identify and disciple your current extravagant givers
- How to develop disciples rather than donors (stewardship is really discipleship)
- How to create a culture of consistent giving (and avoid the up-and-down cycle that comes with holidays, summers, snowstorms, or hurricanes)
- How to establish systematic giving so people give every time they are paid
- How to follow up effectively with those who give (You are following up, right?)
- How to hold people, especially your leaders and staff, accountable for their tithe
- How and when to preach on giving (and how to do it in a way that people will welcome . . . and even want to invite their friends)
- How to discipline members who aren't growing in their giving
- How to create effective giving statements (and how to get people to open them!)

- How to cast a vision that encourages heartfelt stewardship
- How to cultivate big givers (and how not to!)
- How to model generosity in your own life

A healthy stewardship system is integral to a healthy church. To say it another way, you will never have a healthy church if you don't have a healthy stewardship system. A church is made up of its disciples. If those disciples are not spiritually healthy, it's impossible for the church to be healthy. A proper understanding of stewardship and its application are essential elements of every believer's spiritual growth. We train our people to spend time in the Word, to pray, and to share their faith, but we often miss the crucial element of giving. We are all commanded to honor God through our wealth (Prov. 3:9). If we don't disciple our people in that truth, we stunt their spiritual development—which ultimately stunts the growth and ministry of the church. Stewardship is certainly not something to be approached lightly.

The churches I've coached through this system have seen an average 33 percent increase in giving. Many have seen their giving double.

I look forward to the journey we are about to take together. Before we get started, let me recommend a few ways you can set yourself up for stewardship success:

1. *Thoroughly read and digest* Maximize. Grab a highlighter and work your way through the following pages. Make notes in the margins. Go to www.MaximizeBook.com and take advantage of all the free materials that complement what you

are reading. Argue with me; raise an eyebrow. All I ask is that you fully engage in the pages ahead. Think deeply about God's financial plan for his church and your role in that plan.

Commit to finishing what you start. I know how easy it is to grab a book, read the first few chapters, and then toss it aside. With *Maximize*, that would be a mistake. Several of the system's most intriguing concepts don't take form until you've made some progress—concepts such as:

- changing your offering envelopes to postage-paid envelopes
- doing a tithe challenge to create a large percentage of new tithers
- setting up successful online giving
- engaging your big donors in the right way

2. *Study this book with your staff and other key leaders in your church.* The Maximize system is a system that truly begins with you, your staff, and your key leaders. The principles contained in the following pages are principles you all need to understand and commit to if you are going to put a God-honoring stewardship system in place. So get your leaders on board with you right here at the beginning. Let them know how important this information is to pursuing God's plan for your church. If you read *Maximize* as a team, you will reap the benefit of having everyone on the same page (no pun intended!) as you begin to put the system to work.

3. *Be open to new ideas.* Challenge some of the traditional stewardship thinking we've all fallen into. Stay locked in when

something comes up that pushes you past your comfort zone. Keep digging. God has a plan for resourcing his church; it's time we all began discovering that plan and putting it into action. As always, I may challenge familiar concepts but never Scripture essentials.

4. *Get started right away.* Start taking action steps as soon as you learn something helpful. You can act on many pieces of the Maximize system without having the entire structure in place. When you come across one of those pieces, don't sit on it. Act! Decide to start taking your church's stewardship to the next level right now.

What you are about to discover has the potential to revolutionize the current financial state of your church—both corporately and on the level of each individual who comprises it. My prayer is that by the time you finish the last page of this book, you will be ready to step into God's perfect plan for growing his disciples and fully resourcing his work. Let's get started!

stewardship

Becoming a Fully Developing Follower of Jesus

1

shining the light

Illuminating a Taboo Subject

It is impossible to become a fully developed follower of Jesus without also becoming a fully developed steward of your resources.

Randy Alcorn

Wherever your treasure is, there the desires of your heart will be also.

Jesus (Matt. 6:21 NLT)

Over the years, I have heard many pastors tell a common story, often in slightly different forms, to illustrate the relationship between human beings, our possessions, and our God. The story, in its various evolutions, generally involves a sweet treat and centers on the inescapable truth that we tend to take ownership of the things we want—the things our hearts desire—even when they don't actually belong to us. Imagine my surprise when, a few years ago, a scenario played out in my own life that perfectly reflected the heart behind this often-used teaching tool. Since then, I have shared this story with my congregation and with other leaders many times. It always strikes a nerve. I am continually amazed by how God works the circumstances of our lives together for his glory, and I'm thankful he gave me such a fitting story of my own to tell. It goes like this:

On a crisp spring day a few years ago, I took my nephew, who was about eight at the time, to a baseball game. As the fourth inning wound down, he turned to me and said, "Uncle Nelson, can I have some Skittles?" Well, I love my nephew, and I want to grant him the desires of his heart, so of course I said yes. I pulled a couple of dollars out of my pocket, put them in his eager little hand, and watched as he walked the short distance to the concession stand. A few minutes later he returned, already digging hungrily into the bag of candy.

Watching him eat those Skittles brought out my sweet tooth. So I asked him, "Can I have a few of those?"

Without hesitating, he answered, "No, Uncle Nelson, they're almost gone."

Though I didn't say it aloud, I have to admit my instinctive response was, "Look, kid, I gave you the money for those Skittles. Not to mention I am a lot bigger than you are. If I wanted to, I could take the whole bag of Skittles away from you right now." Instead, I let him continue eating his Skittles in silence.

As I sat there listening to my nephew chew and watching him wipe red, yellow, and green coloring off his mouth with his shirtsleeve, I couldn't help but think about how often I have watched people within the church—myself and other leaders included—treat God the same way this child had just treated me. How often have we taken the resources and gifts God has given us and set about consuming them, with little regard for his ultimate ownership? And how often has he looked on, refraining from using his position and power to force us into obedience?

A Taboo Subject

Perhaps I did the right thing by keeping my mouth closed about the Skittles, but when it comes to money within the church, silence is one of our biggest problems. As church leaders, most of us are scared to death to broach the subject of personal or corporate finances with our regular attenders and members. We are hesitant to talk too loudly or too often about biblical stewardship. We are afraid we might offend the faithful or scare off newcomers. We know much of the world sees the church as a money-hungry institution, and we certainly don't want to perpetuate that negative view. Consequently, we are wrapped in a shroud of anxiety.

But who can blame us? For centuries, the church has been on the losing end of a battle over money waged by our enemy. The confusion surrounding the almighty dollar and its place in our lives and ministries is one of Satan's greatest tools for keeping the church as a whole and Christ followers individually from living up to their purpose and potential. Satan does not want the church talking about money, because then the truth of God's plan for abundance might be revealed. Satan's goal is to make stewardship a taboo subject; he wants it to stay in the dark. If we observe the evidence around us, we can see he has largely succeeded. Corporately, churches always seem to be behind budget— always having to say no to opportunities God presents because there's not enough money. Individually, the majority of leaders and congregants are in debt, struggling to make ends meet month to month. Do you think that's how God intends for us to live? Do you think that's how God intends for his church to operate? Always in need? Always in want? Often unable to reach new people and expand the kingdom because of our limited resources?

The answer is a resounding no. To the contrary, God has put a specific plan in place for fully resourcing his church and leading his people out of financial repression. Let this heartening reality sink in: every dollar you need to do ministry is in the pockets of your people. The issue is how you secure those dollars and put them to their proper use. It is your responsibility to lead your people down the path of biblical stewardship so their resources can be released for both kingdom expansion and their own spiritual development—two things that clash with our enemy's intentions. In an attempt to keep such financial truth suppressed, he uses darkness, misconception, and fear to paralyze us. He plants seeds of negativity in the world about the church's relationship with money. He keeps us from being able to fulfill God's purposes. He silences us, as we and our people stumble along in bondage, with our

Skittles tucked tightly in our pockets, our mouths stained from consumption.

Have you noticed that we can talk about almost anything in church these days except money? We can dig into controversial topics of every kind and expose all sorts of things to the light. We allow our people to bring egregious sins into the open so healing can begin, but have you ever tried asking one of those people how much money he makes? Or how much she gives? The thought is laughable. Why? Because money remains in the dark. Somehow, it's more personal than just about anything else.

At The Journey, we aren't afraid to teach on highly uncomfortable subjects. For example, every year we do a four- to six-week series that deals with relationships and sex.

Every dollar you need to do ministry is in the pockets of your people.

A few years ago, we titled this series Desperate Sex Lives. Over the course of six weeks, we talked about things such as dealing with dirty laundry from the past, finding a godly mate, and how to handle the difficulties of being single in the city. As part of these discussions, we hit on some difficult topics. We took a strong biblical look at what God says about homosexuality. We brought the prevalent issue of pornography out of the shadows and looked at it through the lens of truth. Not easy things to stand up and talk about! But for some reason, even issues surrounding something as intimate as sex are less intimidating for most pastors to tackle than issues of money.

From a spiritual perspective, we understand that when someone is caught up in a sin, that sin has to be brought into the light before it can be dealt with. The darkness hates the light because the light has the power to bring freedom. We come into the light when we agree with God. As long as Satan can keep us from understanding—and therefore agreeing with—what God says about money and how we should teach about it, the entire subject will stay tied to his strongholds. People will not understand what God requires of them in their giving, so they will never be able to fully mature in their own relationships with Jesus, and the church will never be able to be properly financed. That is, unless we can break this cycle. We can decide together to enter into the light of truth and then shine it on the subject of money.

Stewardship Is Discipleship

Jesus was never afraid to talk about money. Outside of the kingdom of God, stewardship was his favorite subject. He talked more about money and possessions than about faith and prayer combined. He spent more time dealing with denari than with heaven or hell. In fact, if we were to teach about money as much as Jesus did, we would have to make it our topic every third Sunday. Why? Because Jesus knew that this issue of money and possessions has the power to consume and derail us more quickly than anything else. He doesn't mince words when, in Matthew 6:21, he says, "Wherever your treasure is, there the desires of your heart will be also" (NLT). A fundamental connection exists between a person's spiritual life and his attitude toward money and possessions.

Unfortunately, most church leaders do not have a deep enough understanding of the theology of stewardship to be able to teach about it with conviction. We tend to tuck money away in its own little box and push it to the side, while we focus on people growing in other areas of spiritual maturity. But proper stewardship is an essential element of every believer's growth. We have to learn to talk about it as naturally as we talk about growing in Christ, loving our neighbor, serving God, or sharing our faith. I've heard Randy Alcorn, who has written two highly popular books on this subject (*The Treasure Principle* and *Money, Possessions, and Eternity*), contend, "I've never seen a mature Christian who was not also a mature steward. Giving is part of growing." I fully believe that all people who give in a God-honoring way are growing in their faith and becoming more the people God created them to be. Based on that belief, consider with me one major assumption and three minor assumptions that will underlie what we discuss in the pages ahead.

Major assumption: it is impossible to become a fully developing follower of Jesus without also becoming a fully developing steward of financial resources. (Again, where your treasure is, there your heart will be also.)

When we let this biblically based major assumption influence our thinking, it will begin to permeate the theology, sociology, and culture of our churches. Only then will we start seeing big changes in the area of stewardship and overall discipleship. Here's some good news: in the raging war around stewardship, we have a powerful ally on our side—the Holy Spirit. Too often, the small attempts we do make at stewardship are made in our own strength, without regard to the significant role of the Holy Spirit. But if we are talking about an element of spiritual development here—and I believe we are—we can't divorce the Holy Spirit from the issue.

A giving heart is ultimately up to the working of the Spirit. Just as we can't force anyone to turn his or her life over to Jesus, we can't force anyone to tithe. In matters of salvation, we do our best to present the gospel as clearly and relevantly as possible, but the prompting is up to the Holy Spirit. So it is with stewardship. We do have a major responsibility: we have to develop an understanding of the theology of stewardship; we have to bring the subject of money into the light; we have to motivate and point people toward the truth. But we also have to trust the Spirit to work. We may be able to "convince" people to give once or twice, but when the convincing ends, they will stop giving. On the other hand, if we cooperate with God to move them along a path of discipleship, in the power of the Holy Spirit, we will see great fruit begin to sprout. This leads me to the first of my three minor assumptions.

***Minor assumption 1*: our church members are poorly trained on the foundations of biblical stewardship.**

When it comes to the truth about stewardship, a big, black hole of ignorance hangs over our people's heads. They don't know what they don't know, and we aren't doing the best job of enlightening them. As part of the Maximize system, I will detail a plan for helping people grow in financial knowledge and accountability. We will talk in depth about creating an atmosphere of generosity that models corporate stewardship as it cultivates individual stewards.

On a side note, as you begin implementing the system we will discuss, I want to encourage you to start using your members' level of stewardship as a means of gauging their spiritual growth. Unlike some of the other spiritual disciplines we talk about so often, such as daily time in the Bible and prayer, stewardship is something we can teach and then track. We can observe the extent to which our people digest and apply the teaching. We can train our people on immersing themselves in Scripture, but we have no idea whether they really are. We can exhort prayer until we are blue in the face, but we have no way to measure the health of someone's prayer life. We can never really know how often, or how effectively, people are sharing their faith with their friends.

Stewardship, however, gives us a unique opportunity to keep our finger on the pulse of someone's spiritual development. When we see someone growing in how much they give, this generally implies a step of spiritual growth. If someone who has given sporadically at best begins tithing faithfully, we know God is working in their life. This gauge also works the other way. If someone who used to give faithfully has stopped giving, we can be sure something is wrong. At The Journey, my staff and I have been able to head off potential heartaches and problems before they hit by checking in on someone whose giving had dropped significantly. Now, this is not a black-and-white sign, but it is a good thing to keep your eye on.

The interesting thing about discipleship is that people can be very mature in one area and still immature in another. I'm sure you have run into those who are extremely mature in biblical knowledge but have not given a dime in twenty years. Or you may find people who are mature in the area of finances but are immature when it comes to relationship practices. Obviously, this is a sliding scale. But taken for the measurement it is, keeping up with your people's level of stewardship will prove to be a helpful tool in knowing where their hearts are. The practice of monitoring giving levels also provides us with a clue to how well we are educating and equipping.

Minor assumption 2: **teaching pastors often fail to talk about corporate stewardship because they are poor personal stewards.**

In working with thousands of church leaders over the last decade, I have become convinced that one of the biggest reasons churches struggle with money is because many pastors are poor financial stewards of their own resources. We are called to be godly managers of our households, but most of us focus the bulk of that management energy on being good spouses and good parents. We conveniently ignore truths such as, "The borrower is servant to the lender" (Prov. 22:7). We don't like to dissect how we are managing our houses financially, even though our actions have a direct impact on our churches. If we aren't careful, our personal stewardship habits can be the lid on our church's stewardship potential.

I learned this lesson firsthand when I moved to New York to start The Journey. Working my way along the ministry track over the preceding few years, I had accumulated some debt. Just after Kelley and I got to New York and began preparing for The Journey's launch, I felt God telling me I should get rid of that debt. I had this unshakable sense that I couldn't start and lead a new church with zeal if I was enslaved to creditors. I wasn't excited by this revelation. I had just moved to the most expensive place in the country, and I had sacrificed all of my savings and most of my possessions for the privilege. But God was insistent. So I put together a thirty-six-month plan for getting my financial house in order. God blessed my humble effort so greatly that Kelley and I were out of debt within eighteen months. (For the full audio teaching on my thirty-six-month plan, visit www.MaximizeBook.com for the free "Debt-Free Pastor" download.) In sharing my story with other pastor-friends, I realized I wasn't the only one who had dealt with debt. The truth is that most pastors could use some help in this area. So, church leader, I challenge you to take a hard look at your financial health. Here's one thing I know: until we have our own finances under control, we won't be able to shepherd our people into biblical stewardship with any conviction or integrity.

Minor assumption 3: stewardship is not donor development.

In the 1980s, 1990s, and early 2000s, much of the stewardship thinking within the church centered on the idea of donor development—that is, learn to solicit big money from the rich people in your church and don't focus too much energy on the middle-class segment. This philosophy, which seeped into the church from the world of secular nonprofit fundraising, stemmed from the belief that people who have a lot of money are much more willing to give than people who are struggling to get by. While that may be true, there's one big problem with this way of thinking: it completely disregards biblical teaching on stewardship as discipleship. Sure, you may end up with loads of money, but you also may end up with no one's heart. The best you'll get from traditional donor development is a well-endowed church that is not growing . . . and that's not God's plan.

The stewardship strategy in this book focuses on developing disciples—at all income levels—rather than donors. Remember our major assumption: *it is impossible to become a fully developing follower of Jesus without also becoming a fully developing steward of financial resources.* We are interested in building up stewards who are in the process of becoming fully developing followers of Jesus, which is the structure God put in place for resourcing his kingdom work. As your people learn to be tithers and eventually extravagant givers, based on a percentage of their income rather than on a dollar amount, they will truly begin to see for themselves how God pours his blessing on those who honor him. Disciples, not donors, can attest with conviction that it is truly more blessed to give than to receive.

> Maximize has helped us create a simple system that gives people the best opportunity to obey God with their giving! Through implementing the Maximize principles, we've seen our tithes and offerings double throughout the course of the last twelve months. By learning to think systemically, we've been able to help people grow as disciples and see our church grow in its capacity to reach those who are far from God in our community.
>
> Andy Wood, Lead Pastor
> South Bay Church, San Jose, CA
> Coaching Network Alumnus

2

the heart of stewardship

Introducing the Maximize System

Giving should be an outward, material expression of a deep, spiritual commitment . . . an indication of a willing and obedient heart.

Larry Burkett

All must give as they are able, according to the blessings given to them by the LORD your God.

Deuteronomy 16:17 NLT

New York City is an expensive place to start a new church. When we started The Journey, we didn't have multimillion-dollar donors. We didn't have an endowment or bankers lining up with checkbooks in hand. We were strapped. In fact, for the first six months, we did monthly services on about $10,000. The budget for our first full year was a whopping $168,000. In a city like New York, that's not saying much. Since we didn't have extra money to go around, we had to be very intentional about how we handled every dollar. As I mentioned in the introduction, some churches around the country had partnered with us. (For a free copy of "Funding Your Church Plant," which deals with how we raised funds early on, visit www.MaximizeBook.com.) But we knew that in four years all financial support was going to end. So the race was on for us to become financially self-sufficient within that time frame—or The Journey would end as well.

I am driven by deadlines. While I knew we had only forty-eight months until all help was gone, the pressure didn't really hit me until the beginning of that fourth year. And when it hit, it hit hard. Thankfully, pressure drives creativity. Or as Plato put it, "Necessity is the mother of invention." Not to mention God's timing for revelation is always perfect. You already know the rest of the story: I went to work creating a prayerful, strategic stewardship plan and quickly started taking steps toward our goal. Six months into the year, we became self-sufficient. How? Through the Maximize stewardship system. Of course, at that time, it wasn't called Maximize. It wasn't even called a stewardship system. God was simply leading us through the development and implementation of a process that teaches people to honor him as he directs in his Word and thereby provides for his church.

The base of our stewardship plan was the revelation that if we could help everyone in our church move to the next level in their personal giving, then we could operate as a fully resourced church. That's the way God set it up. In Malachi 3:8, God says, "Will a man rob God? Yet you rob me. But you ask, 'How do we rob you?' In tithes and offerings." God brought my team and me to the understanding that, as long as we allowed our people to continue robbing God, he could not bless us with the resources to do kingdom work at the level he had called us to. But as we identified where our people stood in terms of their giving, and then helped them to take the next step of obedience, and then the next, we could operate under the blessing of God's complete provision. "Bring the whole tithe into the storehouse," God goes on to say in Malachi 3:10, "that there may be food in my house. Test me in this . . . and see if I will not throw open the floodgates of heaven and pour out so much blessing that you will not have room enough for it."

God is a giving God. He gave us life; he gives us breath; he gave us the earth and all its inhabitants; he gives us purpose; he gives us new mercies every single day. Most importantly, he gave us his Son on a Jerusalem hillside. God withholds no good thing from those who love and honor him. So how could we possibly be stingy with God in the area of our finances, especially when he has gone so far as to ask us to "test him" in this one thing?

We have a deep-seated responsibility to lead our people into the truth of stewardship and to model that truth in our own lives. After all, as Randy Alcorn writes, "Our stewardship of our money and possessions becomes the story of our lives."[2] As we learned in the last chapter, helping people grow in the discipline of giving is a core element of overall discipleship. And if you are going to create a healthy process for discipleship to occur—and thereby have a healthy church—a healthy stewardship system is essential.

S.Y.S.T.E.M.

Those of you who are parents know the awe that comes with holding a newborn baby in your arms. Even though babies are born every day, each one is a miracle—especially to her parents. Think back to the last time you looked at ten tiny fingers and toes or watched a little chest move up and down, drawing breath. By cliché, that baby is a "bundle of joy," but she is also a bundle of something else: perfectly formed, intricate systems that are already working together to keep her alive. Thanks to her tiny circulatory system, her heart is pumping blood through her veins. Thanks to her respiratory system, her lungs are taking in air. Her digestive system is breaking down her mother's milk from the very first drop, and her muscular system is letting her wrap her little hand around her father's finger. Even in a brand-new baby, each of these systems and others are fully developed, fully functioning, and ready to grow with her as she starts her journey toward adulthood.

God is into systems. He organized the universe with systems. He established the measurement of time through a system. And from the beginning, he formed our bodies as a cohesive unit of systems. Adam and Eve—unblemished specimens of God's craftsmanship—were compilations of the systems that caused them to function. They were perfect adult examples of that newborn baby. Without systems humming under the surface, they would not have been able to walk or even breathe. Without their systems, they would have remained unmolded lumps of clay, unable to fulfill the purposes of God. From the beginning, God has put systems to work, providing the mechanics and the platform through which he shows his greatness.

One more thing about Adam and Eve. What is it that we know about them for sure? What was the blueprint God used in creating them? Himself. Genesis affirms that God created man in his own image. Don't miss this: God created beings who function through systems and said that they were created in his own image. Yes, God is into systems.

Paul understood God's affinity for systems. That's why, in trying to help us wrap our minds around how the church should function, he compared the body of Christ to the human body. He aligned the design of the church with the functioning of our own different parts. In Romans, Paul writes, "Just as each of us has one body with many members, and these members do not all have the same function, so in Christ we who are many form one body, and each member belongs to all the others" (12:4–5). Sounds remarkably like how God designed our physical bodies with systems, right? Go back and read the verse again, substituting the word *systems* every time you see the word *members*. Makes perfect sense, doesn't it? All the parts of the body—both the church body and the physical body—work together, allowing us to fulfill God's purposes and plans on this earth. And both of those respective bodies function best through well-developed systems.

A system is any ongoing process that *S*aves *Y*ou *S*tress, *T*ime, *E*nergy, and *M*oney and continues to produce results.

Good systems function under the surface to keep things running smoothly so that you can concentrate on more important priorities. Thankfully, you don't have to think about the fact that your neurological system is allowing you to read and process this information. That system is doing its job impeccably, or you wouldn't be able to understand the words in front of you. But if you began to see a decline in your cognitive ability—if all of a sudden you could not remember or analyze information in the way you always have—you would have to deal with the stress of knowing something was wrong and put a lot of money, time, and energy into figuring out where the breakdown was occurring. We may not be aware of a good system when it is running well, but there is no mistaking when something isn't working as it should.

The same is true in the church. We know the church is a body, so it follows that the church also has systems working beneath the surface. I contend that the church is made up of eight systems: the weekend service system, the evangelism system, the assimilation system, the small-groups system, the ministry system, the stewardship system, the leadership system, and the strategic system. (To learn more about these eight systems, download my free e-book "Healthy Church, Healthy Systems" at www.MaximizeBook.com.)

The stewardship system doesn't stand alone. It cuts across the seven other systems. The way you approach stewardship will influence every area of your church. It will affect your weekend service, act as an assimilation gauge for newcomers, work in concert with your small groups, help you determine your leadership structure, be run in large part by your volunteers, and direct the way you approach your overall strategy.

Stewardship can even be used as an evangelism tool, which causes it to dovetail with your evangelism system. Finances are a huge stressor for people in your community. Most of them are living in bondage to debt. A stewardship system that helps individuals and families gain the right perspective and tools for managing money God's way can be a big draw to people outside your doors. (For more on creating a strong evangelism system, see my book *Ignite: Sparking Immediate Growth in Your Church*, Baker, 2009.)

Maximize is the stewardship system that was developed out of this singular goal: to cultivate first-time givers and move them toward extravagant giving. The Maximize system begins when an identified person gives a first-time gift. Once that happens, the system goes to work to move that person through a three-step process:

Maximize is the stewardship system that was developed out of this singular goal: to cultivate first-time givers and move them toward extravagant giving.

1. Turn a first-time giver into a regular giver
2. Turn a regular giver into a tither
3. Turn a tither into an extravagant giver

Wherever your people are on the stewardship continuum, the Maximize system will help them develop as fully as possible at that level and then move them along to the next level.

The continuum has some built-in flexibility. Some first-time givers may jump directly to tithing without going through the step of becoming a regular giver. That's actually ideal. If someone comes to Christ and immediately understands the

FIGURE 1

Stewardship Continuum

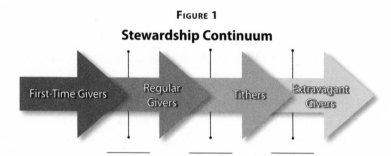

command to tithe, great; we want to move people to tithing as soon as possible. (This is exactly what happened in my own life, as you'll see later.) The step of regular giving is in place, but it is not a necessary stopping point for new givers. Also, some regular givers may move past tithing and jump directly to extravagant giving, if God so stirs their hearts. The flexibility also works the other way. Extravagant givers can slide backward into tithing or less. Tithers can fall back into the early stages of regular giving. So keep in mind that the stewardship scale is a little slippery.

Who Gives?

Back to our story. God made it clear we needed to move people forward in the discipline of giving, but before we could begin, we had to identify where our people presently stood—where they were along the continuum that makes up the current stewardship level in most churches. Every church is made up of five types of givers:

1. never given (non-givers)
2. initial givers (first-time givers)

3. systematic givers (regular givers)
4. proportional givers (tithers)
5. sacrificial givers (extravagant givers)

Non-givers are just that—people who have never given anything to your church, that you know of. This percentage of people is surprisingly high. Your goal with them is simply to get them started—to cultivate a first-time gift. First-time/ initial givers are those people who pop up on your radar because they stick $5 or $10 in an envelope and drop it in the offering. Maybe they've given cash a few times in the past but never in a way that you were able to identify. I like to call these the "God-tippers." They are tipping God. Regular givers are the people who give systematically—once a week, once a month, whenever they are paid, etc.—but their gifts are not proportional to their income. Tithers are those who regularly give 10 percent of their income. They are proportional (and systematic) givers. Extravagant givers are sacrificial givers. They regularly give above and beyond the tithe in a generous, God-honoring way.

With an understanding of these five types of givers, we set to work. You can't get where you want to go if you don't know where you are, so our first step was to put some parameters around these givers. In other words, how were we going to define a regular giver? Since we didn't know the specifics of everyone's income, how would we define a tither? These questions are tricky, and the answers are as unique as each church asking them. But we understood that the key was simply to set amounts to distinguish each level and run with them. That's exactly what we did to get started.

Taking a literal cue from Paul in Philippians 3:14, we drew a racetrack on the whiteboard in our office and asked ourselves, "How are our people doing in this race? Where are they on the track? What do we know?" (See fig. 2.) Then we began prayerfully and studiously to assign dollar amounts to the continuum steps. We decided that people who had given an identifiable gift of $250 or less in the last year fell into the first-time giver category. They had just stepped past the starting line. At that point, they had probably used an envelope to give a few dollars here and there over the course of the year. Next, we labeled those who had given between $250 and $2,000 regular givers. They were about halfway around the track. They may have been giving regularly but certainly not proportionally.

The toughest amount to come up with was the one that identified a tither. Even then our church contained a diverse mix of professionals who made significant incomes and artists

FIGURE 2

Process of Moving 2500 Journey Attenders to Becoming Givers

700 Regular Givers

1425 First-Time Givers

Start Finish

300 Tithers

75 Extravagant Givers

who were struggling to stay afloat in the city. So we decided to give people the benefit of the doubt by choosing a low number. We designated those who had given between $2,000 and $6,000 in the last year tithers. They had the finish line in sight. Lastly, extravagant givers were those who had given more than $6,000. They had burst through the ribbon. Again, we didn't just pick these numbers out of the air. They were strategic guesses based on the makeup of our congregation. As we have grown and changed, the number markers have also grown and changed.

Take another look at the continuum (fig. 1). You'll see three blank lines, one beneath each step of giving. I encourage you to take a few minutes right now and think about the numbers that would correlate with each level of giving in your church. Your numbers may be much higher or much lower than what I've mentioned. I can't stress enough that, in a sense, the numbers are arbitrary. They are simply needed as gauges to help you run your stewardship system. Think of them as the lines that define the parameters of a racetrack. People may move back and forth within those lines, but the lines themselves provide a specified area for the purposes of running the race. Don't get too caught up here. Think about your numbers strategically. Write them down. Move on.

As we examined the financial race our people were running, we saw that most people were at the beginning. Our goal became to move each individual/family unit to the next level and to double their giving over the course of the next year. We began working through questions such as, How do we encourage a non-giver to give for the first time? How do we get those initial givers to start giving regularly? How do we make our regular givers understand the principle of tithing?

And how do we move tithers into the realm of extravagant giving? The Maximize system provided the answer to each of these questions.

I mentioned that we became self-sufficient in three and a half years, but that's just the beginning. Through God's direction and the plan I am going to detail for you, we doubled our weekly giving during that time frame. And the principles we learned still serve us well today. The Maximize system keeps The Journey running year after year as a fully resourced church in the middle of an extravagantly expensive city—one where weekly facility rental alone costs us more than many can imagine. If the Maximize system works in our church environment, it will work in yours. As long as you are willing to cooperate with God to move people into a deeper understanding of his truth—and put the work into setting up a structure for success—you too can become a fully resourced church, able to race toward God's purposes with abandon.

> As soon as I put the Maximize system to work, our church's financial picture began to change. Almost immediately we saw an increase in our weekly giving. We saw sporadic givers move to regular givers, and regular givers become people who were putting God first with their tithe. Our overall giving has increased 60 percent over the same time period a year ago. The vision God has given you can be adequately resourced by the people you are currently reaching!
>
> Jack Ward, Lead Pastor
> Lake Hills Church, Ozark, Missouri
> Coaching Network Alumnus

3

creating a culture
of generosity

"Give, and You Will Receive"

God's work done in God's way will never lack God's supply.

Hudson Taylor

Give, and you will receive. Your gift will return to you in full—pressed down, shaken together to make room for more, running over, and poured into your lap. The amount you give will determine the amount you get back.

Luke 6:38 NLT

Pastor Tim steps into Fictional Community Church's auditorium and glances around. The volunteers are busy setting everything up for the service. The worship team is on stage running through the first song for sound check. The ushers are getting the programs and pens situated in a way that will make them easy to hand out as people enter. The refreshment table volunteers are putting out the coffee and donuts.

Feeling a hungry rumble in his stomach, Tim heads over to the refreshment table to grab a donut. To his surprise, all the donuts have been cut into fourths, with little toothpicks stuck in them. When he spots a sign that says "No seconds" hanging above the table, he knows something is out of whack.

"Hey, guys," Tim says to the two volunteers setting up the coffee. "I'm just wondering why you decided to cut the donuts today," he questions, trying to sound casual.

"Sam asked us to do it that way this morning. Not sure why," answers the younger one.

Tim grabs a speared donut quarter, spots Sam—one of his newest volunteer coordinators—and heads over to find out what's going on.

"Hey, Sam."

"Oh, hi, Pastor Tim! Good morning! How's that donut?" Sam asks with a proud smile.

"Well," says Tim, "honestly, it would be a lot better if I had the whole thing. What's going on with the refreshments, Sam? Why are the donuts cut into pieces?"

"Great idea, right, Pastor Tim? I know we are trying to be extra careful with our money these days, so I thought this would be a good way to cut down on the number of donuts we have to buy."

Pastor Tim puts a friendly hand on Sam's shoulder. "Sam, I appreciate what you are trying to do. I really do. But here's the thing. Cutting back on our refreshments is not the way we want to save money. A big part of the heart behind offering refreshments is to give to people freely . . . to surprise them with our generosity. In a small way, it's a reflection of God's heart."

"Oh, I'm sorry, Pastor," Sam answers, a little embarrassed. "I see what you are saying. I guess I hadn't thought of it that way. I was focusing on trying to cut cost."

"That's understandable, and I do appreciate your concern. There are a lot of areas where we can be more careful with money, but when it comes to giving generously to our people, we always need to keep an abundance mentality."

"Okay! No cutting or toothpicks next week. Oh, and I'll go take down that sign about seconds," Sam says with a slight smile.

"Thanks, Sam. You know, you do a great job here on Sunday mornings. Things wouldn't run nearly as smoothly without you," says Tim. Then with a chuckle he adds, "Hey, you want a donut quarter? I'll walk back over to the table with you. Think I could use a few more myself!"

Can you relate to this scenario as well as I can? You have probably experienced the same tension between generosity toward your people and allegiance to your bottom line— the tension Sam was trying to reconcile even if he was, in his enthusiasm, overstepping his bounds. We often face the temptation to skimp in our giving to our people in the name of saving a dollar. We even spiritualize the decision. We tell ourselves we are "being wise" with our money, saving it for a new ministry initiative or some other worthy endeavor. But the truth is that using our resources to create a spirit of generosity within our churches is one of the wisest financial decisions we can make. Unfortunately, we often approach our people with closed fists instead . . . and then wonder why they are hesitant to give.

The first step in setting the stage for a successful steward-ship system is to create a culture of generosity in your church. Generosity is an often intangible force that trickles down from you to your people and results in specific actions. As your people see you being generous with resources to support them, make them more comfortable, and give them the best opportunity to grow, they will begin to adopt that same spirit of generosity. However, if your actions reflect an attitude of scarcity, your people will act in the same vein and approach giving with a scarcity mentality.

> *Create a culture of generosity in your church.*

Paul convicts us on this point in Romans 2:3–4: "Since you judge others for doing these things, why do you think you can avoid God's judgment when you do the same things? Don't you see how wonderfully kind, tolerant, and patient God is with you? Does this mean nothing to you? Can't you see that his kindness is intended to turn you from your sin?" (NLT). We are quick to judge others for not being faithful in their giving, but we are not always being faithful in the ways we give to them. We are not modeling the outward expression of a generous heart. And yes, we are called to give to our people—sacrificially, even. Another way to think of the word *kindness* in this verse is "generosity." God's generosity draws us into repentance. But how will people ever see or understand God's generosity if we, as the church, fail to model it? God spares nothing for our sakes, as is evidenced by Jesus's death on the cross (John 3:16; Phil. 2:8). And he also promises he will provide for us abundantly (John 10:10). So how can we withhold good things from our people out of fear that we will run out of money?

When I first started Church Leader Insights (www.Church LeaderInsights.com), a training and resource organization for pastors, I did a lot of traveling and consulting with churches across the country. I was often amazed by the things to which churches attached a price tag. I came across churches that charged new believers for new believer Bibles. Other churches charged $0.50 for a cup of coffee before the service. What missed opportunities to till the soil of people's hearts by ministering freely to them! Approaching ministry with such a scarcity mentality robs the church of its chance to show generosity. Not to mention, it also demonstrates a certain lack of faith in what Jesus teaches us in Luke 6:38: "Give, and you will receive. Your gift will return to you in full—pressed down, shaken together to make room for more, running over, and poured into your lap. The amount you give will determine the amount you get back" (NLT). As church leaders, we understand this verse's application in our personal lives, but we often fail to see how it applies to the corporate ministry of the church.

Think again about our enemy's tactics regarding the church and money. He has perpetuated a view of the church in our culture as a money-hungry entity. The average unchurched Joe on the street sees the church as an institution that is always asking people to give. When Joe gets invited to church and actually shows up, quartered donuts and $0.50 coffee only add to his tightfisted view of the church. But we have an opportunity to change that mentality. What if we could wow people with our unexpected generosity, all the while reflecting the depths of God's generous heart? What if your church could become known in your community as the church that gives rather than the church that takes? What a profound impact that would have on creating a culture of generosity within your church and a reputation of generosity beyond your doors.

Since our first days, we have made an intentional decision at The Journey to focus on exemplifying God's provision through generosity. Living with an open hand has not always been easy; we've been stretched. But the rewards of generosity are well worth the effort and expense. We've grown, our people have grown, the church has grown, and the culture of generosity that has been established permeates every area of our ministry. Here are just a few examples of the ways we try to go over and above in modeling generosity:

- We give a free book to all our first-time guests at the service.
- We send a free Starbucks card to all our first-time guests.
  (For the heart and strategy behind free stuff for first-timers, see my previous book *Fusion: Turning First-Time Guests into Fully Engaged Members of Your Church*, Regal, 2007.)
- We offer unlimited coffee and donuts at every service.

- We send a free gift to everyone who gives for the first time.
- We give a free book to everyone who signs up for a fall (campaign) growth group.
- We give free movie tickets to people who bring first-time guests on special occasions.
- We give away free CDs that are relevant to the day's teaching topic.
- We put free resources and materials online.
- We provide free breakfast and/or lunch for our Sunday volunteers.
- We offer free seminary-level classes for all our growth group leaders.
- We put ads in widely read newspapers.
- We do frequent mailings to the community.
- We reach out to hundreds of thousands of people annually through servant evangelism, which involves blanketing the community with free granola bars or bottles of water and postcard invitations to The Journey.

Pastors often ask me, "How do you pay for all of that?" My answer is short and simple: the fruit is in the harvest. I can't afford not to do it. If I refused to foster an atmosphere of generosity at The Journey, I would be cutting off God's blessing and closing down people's hearts. I would be lessening the likelihood that people would visit our church for the first time and then go on to become fully engaged followers of Christ. I don't believe I have the right to short-circuit that opportunity for anyone. Rather, I have a responsibility to give people the best possible opportunity to meet Jesus. Part of that process requires being generous with the resources God gives me to do his work. God is not a God of scarcity. If I am called to be more like his Son and to be his representative on this earth, I certainly can't be a leader of scarcity. Time and time again, God honors the generous seeds we scatter, and The Journey—not to mention the overall kingdom—reaps tremendous fruit.

So before we begin diving into the details of the Maximize system, I want you to examine your heart toward generosity. Refocus your thinking. Shift the paradigm. Ask God to give you wisdom as you begin to walk in the understanding that generosity breeds generosity. Use the lines below to jot down a few ways you can begin modeling God's abundance:

- _____

- _____

- _____

- _____

- _____

- _____

- _____

- _____

- _____

- _____

Now that you have some ideas flowing, let me remind you of two practical steps to take as you start cultivating a generous culture. First of all, begin cutting your spending where you can but not in ways that will visibly influence your generosity. For example, if you are doing mailings, don't stop doing those. Instead, call the printer you are working with and try to negotiate a better rate. Always be on the lookout for internal savings.

Second, focus on proper stewardship. Learn to cooperate with God to bring in the full tithes and offerings. We will spend the rest of our time discovering how to do just that. As we work through the material ahead, I challenge you to view each step through the lens of your own generosity. As church leaders, we set the tone for our people. Every system we implement to make our churches healthier begins with our own obedience to the heart of God. This is especially true with stewardship. By intentionally creating a culture of giving within our churches, we give the Maximize system the air it needs to breathe. Now, on to the details.

initial givers

Raising Up New Givers

4

cultivating first-time gifts

*Practical Ways to Help People Cross
the Threshold*

By nature, the concept of generosity is in direct conflict with
the concept of self-preservation.

Andy Stanley

You must each decide in your heart how much to give. And
don't give reluctantly or in response to pressure. "For God
loves a person who gives cheerfully."

Paul (2 Cor. 9:7 NLT)

Human beings are defined by contradictions. We are full of
duplicity. Day after day we find ourselves in situations that put
our head and our heart in conflict with each other. We usu-

ally know what we should do, but the fear of doing paralyzes us. Paul understood our struggle well, since he admittedly faced it in his own life. In Romans 7:21–24, he laments, "I have discovered this principle of life—that when I want to do what is right, I inevitably do what is wrong. I love God's law with all my heart. But there is another power within me that is at war with my mind. This power makes me a slave to the sin that is still within me. Oh, what a miserable person I am!" (NLT). As long as we are walking this earth, we will be caught in a war that pits our faith in Jesus's ways against the commonsense leanings of our sinful human condition.

Many of this war's confrontations are played out on the battlefield of giving. All human beings—especially those walking in the power of the Spirit—have burgeoning seeds of generosity within them. People like to give. All of us will give something to someone at sometime, regardless of our own financial circumstances or core beliefs. Yet, as real as our desire to give is, we are also subject to a gripping fear that if we give we won't have enough for ourselves. In *Fields of Gold*, Andy Stanley writes, "Fear has always been one of the principal enemies of a growing faith. It has a way of clouding our thinking and obscuring the facts. You may know precisely how God would like you to handle your finances, but fear has the potential to freeze you in your tracks or send you down another path."[3] Fear keeps people locked in the lie of the scarcity mentality—the idea that the more I give away, the less I will have for my own needs.

Added to the equation is the fact that the vast majority of Americans live paycheck to paycheck. They spend every dollar they have just trying to make ends meet. They work to keep the utilities turned on, their kids in clothes that fit, food on the table, and the credit card bills paid. To make matters worse, society has made it the norm for people to spend money they don't have to buy things they don't need to impress people they don't even like. Everyone wants to secure more of the pie for themselves, even if it means mortgaging their lives. No matter how many seeds of generosity are sprouting within average Americans, the reality of the economic climate and the voice of common sense tells them to clutch their wallets with all their might. Even though their hearts may tend toward giving, their heads try to shut down the impulse before any money makes its exit.

Into this tangled web of misconception, debt, generosity, darkness, willingness, contradiction, and confusion steps the earnest church leader ready to pursue God's passion for proper stewardship. You have quite a responsibility on your shoulders. God has put you in the position to hold up his truth about financial management. You have the answers that can free people's hearts from the stress of economic straits and open their eyes to a life of abundance. You can help your people discover the truth that God owns everything they have and that their responsibility is simply to manage it. You have the key to unlock the floodgates that keep your church from being fully resourced, the way God intends. You can foster the seeds of generosity that God has planted in your people's hearts.

What's your first step? How do you get people who want to give but are scared to give to understand the significance of investing in the work of the church? How do you help those people in your congregation who have never given anything to take the first step of giving? How do you move them onto the continuum that will lead them toward extravagant giving? By doing all you can to take out the artillery that is fighting against God's purposes. You have to diffuse fear by helping your people's intellects match the cry of their hearts. The first step to cultivating givers in your church is to educate people regarding the biblical basis of giving—first, by teaching stewardship during your weekend service; second, by teaching that the church's ministry is supported by its members; and third, by educating your people on the various options for giving available to them.

The Weekend Service

Start by educating your people regarding the biblical basis of stewardship during your weekend service. The large majority of your congregation has no idea what the Bible says about giving. And many of those who think they know a thing or two are misinformed. As long as your people remain ignorant on the topic, they won't have a fair opportunity to develop into stewards. Your weekend service gives you the perfect opportunity to educate your people. You can illustrate the biblical basis for stewardship in four ways.

The first step to cultivating givers in your church is to educate people regarding the biblical basis of giving.

1. Stewardship Teaching Four Times Per Year

People are searching for financial truth. If they think you have valuable insight to offer, they will listen. And you do have valuable insight to offer—the most valuable insight available, as a matter of fact. So you should never shy away from preaching on stewardship. We need to adopt the boldness Jesus had in teaching on money and possessions. He understood that a person's heart is tied directly to his or her checkbook. Since Jesus was interested in the hearts of men and women, he had no choice but to take a direct interest in their dealings with money—and neither do we.

I suggest teaching on stewardship at least four times every year. Once per quarter, step up to the plate to challenge and educate your people on becoming fully developing stewards of kingdom resources. My experience shows that two of those four times should be as follows:

- *Teach on money in mid to late January.* Strategically speaking, it is important to plan the first stewardship message of the year around the second or third weekend of January. Your people will be recovering from the Christmas rush. Yet, even as they begin relaxing in the new year, the bills will start filling their mailboxes, letting them know just how much they spent in the name of that holly, jolly celebration. They are going to be thinking about what the year ahead holds and what changes they need to make. New Year's resolutions will be fresh in their minds. This is a perfect time to teach on issues of budgeting, debt, and how to get your financial house in order.

- *Teach on money right after "back to school."* The beginning of the school year is the other natural period when people pause to organize their lives. There are new schedules and new routines. The crisp, fall air brings a call to order of sorts. Depending on the part of the country you are in, this may be in August or September. Whatever the actual date, just make sure you slate the teaching for a week or two after everyone gets back into the swing of scheduled living so that the majority of your regular attenders will be there . . . and eager to hear all you have to say.

These two times of year are when people are feeling the most financial pressure. They are concerned about how they are handling their money; they are looking for some guidance. Too often, we feel like we are pushing financial teaching on our people, but that's not the case. That feeling comes from our own insecurity in dealing with the subject. In reality, our people want to hear biblical truth about the currency that is so apt to control their lives. Don't buy the enemy's lie that your people are resistant to teaching that deals with money. They aren't. By and large, they are longing for even more of it. (For free downloads of financial sermons I've preached at these two important times of year, visit www. MaximizeBook.com.)

The other two stewardship Sundays during the year are up to your discretion. I usually like to do something around Easter and then again in the summer. Feel out what works best with the flow of your calendar. What's most important is not when you preach on money but that you do preach on money.

On a side note, you can position a Sunday that you will be teaching on stewardship as a "big day" within your church and use it as an opportunity to reach out to the community. (To learn more about spurring evangelism through "big days," see *Ignite: Sparking Immediate Growth in My Church*, Baker, 2009.) Financial issues are important to everyone. Unchurched people are also searching for revelation about how to manage their resources, and if you invite them, they will likely come to hear what you have to say, which gives you a great opportunity to connect them to your church. Don't minimize the position you've been given to speak truth into people's lives, including the people currently beyond your doors.

2. *Stewardship Testimonies Two Times Per Year*

Personal stories have the ability to touch listeners in a powerful way. While your preaching can educate people and give them many of the tools they need to begin taking steps of stewardship, personal testimonies from those who have already walked the path can exponentially increase your effectiveness. Let your people hear from someone in the church who has struggled with finances and has seen the blessings that come with intentionally deciding to honor God despite the struggle. Let them hear from someone who could be considered wealthy but who has learned the truth about want versus need and how to live with a heart toward God's abundance. The greater the variety of testimonies, the greater the number of individuals who will be influenced.

I suggest presenting short stewardship testimonies at least two times every year. At The Journey, we usually keep testimonies to four minutes. That's all it takes to touch someone's heart in a powerful way. I fully believe that, outside of the sermon, testimonies are the single greatest element that can be used in a Sunday service to speak to people where they are and encourage them to take steps toward God. The people in your congregation who are hesitant to give will be moved by the stories of people who have discovered the joy of giving. They will see their worries and excuses reflected back to them and overcome. Often, these testimonies are the tipping point that leads to a first-time gift.

3. Giving Challenges Two Times Per Year

We are wired to respond to challenges. Innately, we know that challenges are what cause us to grow. One of the most effective ways to cultivate first-time gifts from non-givers is to boldly challenge them to start giving. I suggest putting forth first-time giving challenges at least twice every year.

The best way to introduce a giving challenge is to tie it in with one of your messages or testimonies on stewardship. Turn your people's attention to the idea of honoring God through their finances, and then immediately encourage them to give for the first time. A good giving challenge is attached to a timetable. For example, after a message on giving or some other applicable scenario, challenge your people who have never given to start by giving something consistently over a set period of time. At this point, you are not looking for a percentage/proportional gift. You are simply challenging them to give something every week for the next eight weeks, or whatever your time frame may be.

Another way to set up a giving challenge is to tie it to a churchwide study or preaching series. For example, last fall we did a churchwide study called The New Testament Challenge. As part of the study, I encouraged our people to read through the New Testament in three months. The time-bound nature of this campaign gave me a great opportunity to challenge people to give for the first time. (For more on The New Testament Challenge spiritual growth campaign, see www. MaximizeBook.com.) As part of the teaching, we reminded people that if they were not growing in giving, they were not growing. Then we challenged everyone to give regularly over the course of the three-month study. The amount of the gift was not important. For some, it may have been $40 every week of the three months, while for others it may have been $14 or $400. The point was just to get them started.

As church leaders, we are never shy about challenging our people to read the Bible through in a year or to share their faith with their friends. There is no reason we should be hesitant to challenge people in their giving either. Giving is a spiritual discipline that is necessary for their growth and development as followers of Jesus. Challenging people to honor God through stewardship is part of what we are called to do.

4. Stewardship Resources—Continuously

Resources give you the opportunity to offer your people an ongoing stewardship education. While you may preach on proper stewardship only four times each year or present testimonies and giving challenges twice, you can make stewardship resources available year-round. In the last chapter, we talked about creating a culture of generosity. Continually giving your people access to free CDs to help them with their financial concerns is an ideal way to perpetuate that generous culture.

Every Sunday at The Journey, we offer free CDs at our resource table. These CDs are on all sorts of topics, but the ones people gravitate to the most are related to stewardship. We have CDs on getting out of debt, living on a budget, dealing with financial crisis, and managing God's wealth, among other things. People take these CDs by the dozens every week. Producing them is a negligible cost for us, and they allow our people to engage continually in stewardship education.

Another way to make financial resources available to your people is through your website. We regularly post articles and tools at www.journeymetro.com to help move people into a deeper understanding of their stewardship responsibility. We post MP3s similar to the CDs at the resource table, so if people don't want a CD, they can just download an MP3 to their iPod and listen anytime. We offer downloadable budget sheets, debt worksheets, and tithe calculators. People need these tools to get their finances under control as God desires, so we do our best to make them as accessible as possible. (For samples of these resources, including sermon MP3s, visit www.MaximizeBook.com.)

Ministry through Members

Misconceptions about how the church is funded have permeated most people's thinking. You would be shocked by how many people sitting in your congregation don't know that the ministry of the church is made possible because of their giving. They are under the false impression that someone else is paying the bills. They think there is some sort of denominational stipend, some trust fund, or some long-lost elder who foots the expenses. Obviously, we know that none of these things is true. The church is able to operate because of the tithes and offerings of its members. That's the way God set it up.

So as part of educating your people regarding the biblical basis of stewardship, you have to educate them on the fact that their giving is integral to the church's existence. The three most effective ways to do this are:

1. *Through the Sunday service.* Take advantage of the opportunities you have during your service to remind people of the part they play in making your church's ministry a reality. Every Sunday at The Journey, while we receive the offering, we say something along the lines of, "The Journey is a member-supported church. Everything we do is made possible through your faithful giving." (More on that in the next chapter.)

Another opportune time to remind people of the significance of their involvement is during baptism. During your baptism service, make sure to point out that God uses the ministries of the church in a powerful way to draw people to himself. Thank your people for being faithful in supporting the church and remind them that their faithfulness went a long way toward making baptism a reality for everyone being baptized that day. Let them know they have played a part in what they are about to witness. This powerful realization will stir them to even greater generosity.

2. *Through small groups.* When you do your small-group leader training, take a few minutes to remind people how the church is resourced. As you add to your leaders' knowledge, encourage them to relay that knowledge to their group members.

3. *Through ministry teams.* The volunteers on your ministry teams see offering money at work at close range. Regularly remind them where the equipment and supplies they are working with come from. For example, if you buy a new piece of equipment for your media team, encourage the leader of the media team to dedicate that equipment to God in the presence of his volunteers. Ask him to talk about the fact that the equipment doesn't belong to them but to God—and that it was paid for with kingdom money. Such knowledge will change their perspective on and handling of the equipment, and it will encourage them to think about how their own level of stewardship is helping to support the ministry of the church.

These are just three of many ways to remind your people that ministry happens because they give. Be creative in taking every opportunity that presents itself. When we make this kind of discussion part of the fabric of the church, people realize the significance of giving. Having a clear understanding of where their money goes will encourage people toward stewardship.

Options for Giving

Finally, educate your people regarding the various options for giving. We'll discuss this in detail in part 3, so I'll address it just briefly here. The fact is not everyone who calls your church "home" is going to be there every Sunday. As much as we would like our people to be in church every week, it just doesn't happen. When you are trying to gauge how many attenders you truly have, look at how many different people attended your church over the course of a six-week period. Twelve hundred people may have attended last Sunday, but over the course of six weeks, you may have had more than twenty-five hundred different attenders who consider your church their home church.

If we are offering people the opportunity to give only at the Sunday service, we could be cutting our tithes and offerings in half. We would be remiss to let our people's giving be tied to something as unpredictable as attendance. What if someone is in church but forgets his checkbook? What if there's a sick child in the family, so everyone stays home? What if there's a snowstorm in your area? What if it's an unusually beautiful day and several of your couples head to the lake? You can't always predict or control your people's attendance, but you can regulate their giving whether they are in church or not.

Our job is to develop better disciples, and stewardship is a significant part of this. In turn, we need to make sure we are giving people the best possible opportunity to be strong stewards, regardless of the weekly issues they may face. The key is to provide various ways to give—and then make sure your people understand the options. This is one area of discipleship where we can ensure our people are being faithful. Again, we will dig into this shortly. For now, just remember that educating your people on their options for giving is an essential part of educating your people regarding the biblical basis of stewardship.

Your heart's cry for your people should be that they are continually growing into fully developing followers of Jesus. As you demonstrate this desire to see them grow by investing in their stewardship education, you will be equipping them to honor God through cheerfully giving back to the kingdom. As Andy Stanley goes on to say, "When you begin to view your wealth from God's perspective, you'll see that the thing to fear isn't giving away too much, but sowing too little."[4] Education is a necessity for helping your people gain God's perspective. Put the vision of true stewardship before them and then show them why and how to pursue that vision. As you do, their knowledge and faith will increase, their fear will decrease, and the Spirit of God will begin moving them into the realm of active generosity.

5

easy does it

Eliminating Unnecessary Barriers to Giving

Good things that cannot be calculated or quantified are set in motion in your life and in your finances when you give.

Dave Ramsey

Take from among you a contribution to the LORD; whoever is of a willing heart, let him bring it as the LORD's contribution: gold, silver and bronze.

Exodus 35:5 NASB

You may have heard the famous anecdote about how people catch monkeys in India. Long ago, an insightful hunter figured out that monkeys are selfish creatures, so he created a method of capture that takes advantage of that nature.

First, the monkey hunter cuts a small hole in one end of a coconut—a hole just big enough for the monkey to fit his hand in—and ties a long cord to the other end. Then he puts peanuts, banana chunks, or some other enticing treat into the hole, places the coconut in the monkey's path, and sneaks away, holding the other end of the cord. Inevitably, an unsuspecting monkey comes along, sniffs out the treat, and wriggles his little hand into the hole to grab the treasure. With that, the hunter's job is done. All he has to do is yank his side of the cord, and the entire monkey/coconut kit and caboodle lands at his feet.

But isn't something missing here? Why wouldn't the monkey just pull his hand out of the coconut and run for his life? Remember that monkeys are selfish. Once they get their hands on something they want, they won't let go. With his fist wrapped around the goods, the monkey can't get his hand out of the hole. If he would just loosen his grip and let go of the bounty, he could save himself. But he clings tightfisted to what's "his" and finds himself ensnared . . . even unto his own demise.

It's easy for us to see how ridiculous the monkey is being. If we were sitting at the edge of the jungle watching the scenario play out, we would scream, "Let go! That little fortune isn't worth your life!" And yet back in our own corner of the world, we are guilty of approaching our money and possessions the same way the monkey approaches those peanuts and banana chunks. We hold on too tightly. We want what is ours, and we want it so badly that we are often blind to the consequences of our grasping. Author Gary Thomas observes, "One of the greatest spiritual challenges for any Christian is to become less self-absorbed. We are born intensely self-focused."[5] We are born keen on self-preservation and self-promotion. Despite the seeds of generosity that may be in our hearts, we—and the people in our congregation—are prone to approach life with a hoarding mentality. We want to be secure. We want to get all we can. We are focused so intently on our "treasure" that we don't see the hunter lurking behind a nearby tree.

How can you and I as church leaders begin to change this mentality? How do we open people's eyes to the truth of God's plan for their provision and their giving? As we saw in the last chapter, education is key. But we also have to develop an offering process that makes it easy for people to give. While educating people regarding the significance of stewardship will help them begin loosening their death grip, that education won't go very far if we don't provide a nonintimidating, well-thought-out plan for helping them take the step of giving for the first time. We can't just stand to the side and yell for them to run toward the life that giving brings. We have to help them open their hands.

The Easy Offering

The Maximize system begins when someone gives an identifiable gift for the first time. You can't track or disciple people if you don't know they are giving, so it's critical that you create an environment in which givers make their gifts identifiable. For our immediate purposes, this means you provide them with an easy-to-use envelope as part of a thoughtful offering process. How much intentional planning have you put into your offering process? In coaching countless churches on stewardship, one of the most consistent mistakes I see is a poorly planned offering procedure. Churches leave huge amounts of kingdom money in the auditorium every Sunday simply because they don't conduct the offering in a way that allows every giver—and especially first-time givers—to give.

Recently, Kelley and I visited an out-of-town church. Everything about the service was phenomenal. I hadn't walked into the church planning to give, but I was so encouraged by the work they were doing that I decided to give a small gift to show my support. When the pastor mentioned that the offering bucket was going to be passed in a couple of minutes, I began fumbling through my program to find the offering envelope. That's when things took a turn for the worse. Just as I started to fill out the envelope and get my gift ready, the pastor asked us to stand and sing. The lights in the auditorium went down—way down.

So there I was, trying to get my gift into the envelope, figure out how to seal it, and finish filling out the requested information on the front, while standing in the dark and feeling the pressure to sing. Then all of a sudden, Kelley was holding the offering bucket. I wasn't ready, so I had to let it pass me by. People were waiting down the line, and I didn't want to be the guy holding up the process. Nobody does. So even though I wanted to give and tried to give, the church's offering procedure kept me—and who knows how many others—from being able to give. And I'm a pastor. I teach this stuff. I am more than familiar with the way offerings are received. If I couldn't get a gift in that bucket, imagine the unschooled first-timer who had decided to give.

Unfortunately, this scenario is all too common. One of the biggest reasons people don't give to your offering is because they don't know when it is coming and don't have sufficient time to get their gift ready.

Making it easy to give is critical to cultivating first-time gifts. While many of your regular attenders and members may not give at the service, choosing instead to use one of the other giving options we'll discuss later, the overwhelming majority of first-time gifts will be placed directly in the offering bucket. So you need to make things as easy as possible. Don't let the offering be a surprise. Don't distract givers from their decision to give. Here's the guiding goal for an effective offering: give every person who wants to give the opportunity to give. You can meet this goal by:

> *Give every person who wants to give the opportunity to give.*

- providing a larger-than-expected, easy-to-fill-out offering envelope
- mentioning the offering early in the service
- giving people a two-minute warning
- talking during the offering rather than singing a song
- not dismissing people until the offering is completed

At The Journey, we utilize a connection card to communicate with our congregation every week. The card gives us a way to connect with our regular attenders and to collect contact information from new attenders. (I have discussed the connection card in great detail in other books, so I'll spare you here. You can learn all about it in *Fusion: Turn-*

ing First-Time Guests into Fully Engaged Members of Your Church, Regal, 2007.) About twenty minutes into our service, we ask everyone to fill out the connection card, and we make the simple statement that they'll be able to turn in the card when the offering bucket is passed at the end of the service. With this brief comment, we have subtly let people know when they can expect the offering bucket to come around, so they won't be taken by surprise.

Later, as the teaching pastor wraps up his message, he (or another teaching pastor acting as the day's "host") gives people what we call the "two-minute warning." (Note that, depending on the specific day and type of sermon, we may sing a worship song after the message but before the two-minute warning.) He simply lets everyone know the offering will be received momentarily. Then he keeps talking. There is no song and no dimming of lights. He talks about how The Journey is supported by its members; he mentions a couple of the options for giving; he reminds everyone to finish filling out the connection card. As he talks, people who want to give have time to complete the offering envelope, get their gift inside, and make sure they are ready for the bucket. Once the buckets have made the rounds and been collected, we either sing a final song or simply dismiss the congregation. By this time, we are confident we have given everyone who wants to give the best possible opportunity to do so.

The teaching pastor closes his message with a prayer. As he says amen and heads offstage, Pastor Tim walks on with a connection card in his hand. He looks out over the crowd.

"In just a moment we are going to receive our offering," he begins. "So go ahead and finish completing your connection card. If you are a first-time guest with us today, we want to thank you for being here. We have a free gift for you. It's a book called *The Case for Faith* by Lee Strobel. All we ask is that you drop your completed connection card in the offering bucket when it comes around."

Tim pauses for a second. He spots Jon—who was just baptized with his wife, Liz, a few weeks ago—thoughtfully filling out an offering envelope. Liz is watching over his shoulder. Tim continues, "As our offering ushers begin to pass the buckets, let me encourage you to give big. We are a member-supported church, so all the ministry we are able to do here is because of your generous tithes and offerings. If you aren't prepared to give today, don't worry. You can take your offering envelope home with you and mail it back to us with your gift. It's postage paid and comes directly to our office. Or you can give online any time at our website." Tim continues to talk as the buckets are passed.

When the bucket gets to Jon, he carefully places his connection card and offering envelope inside. He glances at Liz, who smiles and gives his shoulder a small squeeze.

Pastor Tim feels he has looked in on a significant moment. Then noticing that the buckets have all been collected, he closes the offering time with, "Before we dismiss, the worship team is going to come back out and lead us in a final song. I invite you to stand and sing."

Notice how Pastor Tim used the two-minute warning to give people plenty of time to find and fill out the offering envelope and get their gift ready. From the minute he stepped onstage and said, "In just a moment we are going to receive our offering," those who wanted to give started getting prepared. He didn't give them the warning and then fill the two minutes with a worship song. No one was asked to stand. Tim intentionally provided an opportunity for people to prepare their gifts before the buckets were passed. By talking during the offering, you give people the time they need to be able to give. Not to mention you also have the opportunity to relay some important information about your church—such as the fact that it is member-supported and other options are available for giving. Also notice Tim used the phrase "receive the offering" rather than "take the offering." This seemingly small difference in terminology makes a large difference in people's perception of stewardship.

Part of receiving the offering in the context of your overall stewardship system is making sure people give an accountable gift. Again, the best way to ensure accountability from first-time givers is to provide a larger-than-expected, easy-to-fill-out envelope. If you aren't using offering envelopes at your church, you have little hope of building a powerful stewardship system.

A few years ago, I traveled south to consult with a fast-growing church plant that had suddenly become stuck. They couldn't figure out why, after such growth, things had cooled off so drastically. I started examining the various areas of the church. I looked at their space, setup, staffing, and the like. At the end of the day, it came down to one little issue:

they did not use offering envelopes. They couldn't identify or disciple stewards, so they were seeing stagnation. You simply can't cultivate givers if you don't know who your givers are.

Here are a few things to keep in mind about offering envelopes. First of all, always include envelopes in your program, even if you hand out boxes or mail them separately to your members. Don't assume they brought one with them, because most don't. Every Sunday, our program contains at least three things: a connection card, message notes, and an offering envelope. Second, make sure the offering envelope is easy to fill out. As an exercise, try sitting down and filling out the envelope on your lap, like your people have to do during a service. Is there enough space provided to fill in the requested information? Are you asking for too much information? Unnecessary information? Examine the envelope through your givers' eyes.

Finally, provide envelopes that are a little bigger than expected. My experience has shown that larger envelopes lead to larger gifts. People don't like stuffing money into tiny little envelopes. They feel they are taking a significant step by giving, and they want that gift to be fully contained. Just as people are not comfortable depositing large amounts of money at an ATM without using an appropriate envelope, they won't be comfortable passing large amounts of money to you if your envelope indicates a lack of thought or preparation on your part. Provide envelopes that are user-friendly, and then challenge your people to use them. That way they'll be accountable for the gift they've given, and you will be able to begin properly leading them down the path of stewardship.

Passing the Plate

Another key element of a strong offering procedure is having an effective process for passing and collecting the buckets (or plates or baskets—whatever you use). When done well, the offering won't take any longer than the two minutes you are allowing. The ushers should be finished by the time you run out of things to say. The process illustrated below is one I initially learned from Rick Warren at Saddleback Church—one they have refined to the point where they can receive the offering in a crowd of over three thousand in about forty-five seconds.

Figure 3

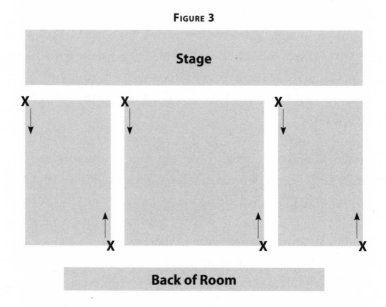

The Xs in figure 3 represent preplaced stacks of buckets. When the host comes onstage at the end of the message and gives the two-minute warning, the offering ushers stand up and get ready. Each one goes to his or her assigned spot and picks up the stack of buckets. When the host gives the cue, "As our offering ushers begin passing the buckets . . . ," each usher begins handing one bucket to the person on the end of each aisle to his or her left. The ushers who start at the front of the room walk toward the back, while the ushers starting in the back of the room walk toward the front, as indicated by the arrows. When an usher runs out of buckets, she begins collecting the buckets that the usher opposite her passed out.

Sometimes pastors question this offering process, feeling like they will interrupt the flow of the service if they spend two full minutes talking about and receiving the offering. This concern goes back to a misunderstanding of biblical stewardship. The offering is part of worship, just as Scripture study and prayer are part of worship. As people prepare their gifts and place them in the offering buckets, they are worshiping God through giving. Pausing to receive the offering is a perfect reminder that there is significant purpose behind the act. We do our people—not to mention God—a disservice if we ask them to give and then quickly move on to a "holier" part of the service. Remember, we are called to shine a light on giving as we develop stewards. Don't cut off your congregation's ability to worship God through their tithes and offerings. Instead, shape your offering process to be a conduit of that opportunity.

Bringing It All Together

An intentional, thoughtful offering process is essential in cultivating first-time gifts and setting people on the stewardship continuum. I have seen church after church increase their giving and identify new givers by paying attention to the details of the offering. I recently worked with a church in Florida that committed to making these changes. Their offering immediately increased by 30 percent. And they are just one of hundreds of examples. While the increase in income is important, the fact that they are now able to identify new givers each week is even more important. Receiving identifiable first-time gifts sets the stewardship system into motion and helps new givers take steps toward regular giving, tithing, and extravagant giving.

We have to work with our people. As a rule, they are not overly eager to loosen the grip they've been taught to have on their money, so the easier we can make it for them to step toward the path of stewardship, the better. When we make it difficult for them to give for the first time—even if we are doing so unintentionally—we are holding the cord that keeps them bound to their possessions. We may have educated them, but our actions serve only to strengthen the strongholds of materialism and bondage in their lives. Part of our job is to help people open their hands and find the freedom that comes with giving. As we create an offering procedure that makes it easy to give for the first time, we take a big step toward releasing them from the snare.

> Our average number of giving units each week was ten to fifteen. Then, as the Maximize system recommends, we took the simple step of putting an envelope in with each of our Sunday bulletins. We are now three months into the implementation of this, and our weekly average has more than

doubled, with thirty-two to thirty-five giving units on a typical Sunday and a 50 percent increase to our weekly offering.

Marty Schmidt
The Bridge, Ottumwa, Iowa
Coaching Network Alumnus

6

revolutionary gratitude

A Little Thanks Goes a Long Way

The reality is that Americans are willing to give more generously than they typically do, but it takes a purposeful and
well-executed approach to facilitate that generosity.

George Barna

The master said, "Well done, my good and faithful servant.
You have been faithful in handling this small amount, so now
I will give you many more responsibilities. Let's celebrate
together!"

Matthew 25:23 NLT

Sometimes the simplest things are the most revolutionary. The
details we overlook have the power to change worlds. Think

about the influence contained in a simple smile, an encouraging word, or a heartfelt thank-you. These niceties can bring down the staunchest defenses. They make people trust us and want to engage with us. No wonder mothers around the globe teach their children to mind their manners. *Please* and *thank you* really are the magic words. So why do we forget the significance of a simple thank-you as we grow older? For one, we are steeped in a culture that neglects thankfulness. Even within the church, we neglect thankfulness. This neglect leads to a spiral of self-centeredness and the kind of selfish attitudes we discussed in the last chapter. But perhaps even more importantly for us as church leaders, it robs us of the opportunity to continue fostering a spirit of generosity.

A Powerful Lesson in Simplicity

I learned the power of a simple thank-you shortly after I gave my life to Christ as a college student in North Carolina. I was trying to uncover all I could about my new faith, and as part of that journey I started listening to Chuck Swindoll on the radio. One day, I decided I would send a gift to the Swindoll ministry. But remember I was a college kid, so it wasn't any grand donation, just a token of gratitude for what I had been learning from the radio ministry. I wrote my meager $20 check, stuck it in an envelope, and sent it off.

Guess what showed up in my mailbox a week or so later? A thank-you note from Chuck Swindoll. More specifically, a thank-you note that told me how my money was being used and an envelope for me to give again. They even included a little book for me to read. I was impressed. I felt a sense of satisfaction knowing my gift had been received and it was being put to good use, which gave me an inclination to continue being generous with their ministry.

Let's fast-forward a couple decades and contrast that experience with an all-too-common first-time giving experience within the church. Recently, I received a blast email from a church with which I'm familiar. I decided to go online and give a small gift. The online giving process went smoothly, but once I had given, I didn't receive any correspondence. Nothing. Not even an email telling me the transaction had been processed. Certainly no thank-you note. I actually had to check my credit card statement a couple weeks later to make sure the transaction had gone through. After a couple months, I did receive a giving statement from the church—a plain, printed giving statement in a windowed envelope. When it first showed up in my mailbox, I thought it was a bill. (We'll discuss effective giving statements in detail in part 3.)

Considering the follow-up experiences I had with these two ministries, which one do you think I would prefer to give to again? Which one do I have more confidence in? The Swindoll ministry, of course. They let me know my gift had been received, thanked me, cast a vision for the future, gave me a free gift, and invited me to give again. While the non-responsive church may be involved in all kinds of significant ministry initiatives and may have put my money to great use, because they failed to communicate that to me, the giver, I lost trust in them.

As I moved through college, then seminary, and eventually became a young church leader, the Swindoll experience stayed with me. I remember asking myself, "Why can't we do this in the church? When people give for the first time, isn't it only right to thank them?" So when we started The Journey, I was determined to put a process in place to follow up with our givers. That process is now a critical piece of the Maximize system.

An effective plan for follow-up underscores and enhances your entire stewardship system in several ways. First of all, the simple yet revolutionary act of sending someone a thank-you note reassures him that his gift has been received and is appreciated, and gives him insight into how it is being used. Second, using follow-up to cast a vision and educate people gives you yet another avenue for training people in biblical stewardship. And third, providing a small, free gift reinforces a spirit of generosity.

An effective plan for follow-up underscores and enhances your entire stewardship system.

A few years ago, the Barna Research Group released a study addressing the low levels of giving among self-professed Christians. As part of their research, they identified five issues that keep people tightfisted:

> Some people lack the motivation to give away their hard-earned money because the church has failed to provide a compelling vision for how the money will make a difference in the world. These are donors who can find other uses for their money and are not excited about simply handing money over to the church. The second group is those who see their giving as leverage on the future. They withhold money from the church because they do not see a significant return on their

investment. The third segment is comprised of people who do not realize the church needs their money to be effective. Their church has done an inadequate job of asking for money, so people remain oblivious to the church's expectations and potential. The fourth group is composed of those who are ignorant of what the Bible teaches about our responsibility to apply God's resources in ways that affect lives. The final category contains those who are just selfish. They figure they worked hard for their money and it's theirs to use as they please. Their priorities revolve around their personal needs and desires.[6]

Effective follow-up—especially when combined with education from the pulpit and a thoughtful offering procedure—has the potential to counter every one of these five issues. Follow-up solidifies your efforts to teach your people about biblical stewardship and to encourage them to give. Plus, it gives you the opportunity to continue discipling your people as you move them along the giving continuum.

Think of follow-up as the great connector. Imagine standing and stretching out one arm in front of you and the other behind you. Your body represents follow-up. Your back arm reaches toward the work you've already done to cultivate a first-time gift, and your front arm reaches forward to connect those first-time gifts to future steps of stewardship. Follow-up brings the two together by serving as both the centerpiece and the conduit of your ability to disciple stewards. It is arguably the most important piece of the Maximize system. Yet it is as simple as a thank-you.

Faithful Follow-up

So you received an initial gift. You've identified the new giver, most likely because she used an envelope but perhaps because she gave online or in one of the other ways we'll discuss. Now what? Now it's time to put your follow-up plan into action. When someone gives to your church for the first time, that's your best opportunity to encourage her to give again. Garnering a second gift is much easier than garnering a first, because the giver's heart has already been opened to give. She has taken a step of faith and released part of her treasure into your hands. What you do from here will determine whether the gift is a one-time flash in the pan or whether the giver will continue to give, grow, and become a fully developing follower of Jesus.

Regular giving is a mark of discipleship. Our goal is to follow up with a course of action that will turn a new giver into a regular giver as quickly as possible. We do that in two complementing ways: initial follow-up and ongoing follow-up.

Initial Follow-up

Initial follow-up is a two-step process. Step 1 is to send a personalized email to every first-time giver by Tuesday of each week (see fig. 4). The main purpose of the email is to thank the person for giving. You can also take advantage of the opportunity to mention that the gift is tax deductible, add to the giver's comfort level by giving a phone number where she can reach you, remind her that giving is part of discipleship, and give her some options for future giving. I always include a

FIGURE 4

To: First-time Givers
From: Nelson Searcy
Subject: The Journey—Thanks for Giving

Hi [first name],

I want to thank you for your financial gift to The Journey this past week. According to our records, this is the first time you have given either online, by check, or by using the Sunday giving envelope.

Thanks for your support and for honoring God through giving. All donations to The Journey are 100 percent tax deductible, and you will receive quarterly updates as well as an end-of-year giving statement next January. If you have any questions about your giving at any time, please don't hesitate to call me.

Regular giving is a mark of a fully developing follower of Jesus. To help you remain faithful in giving, here are four options:

1. Use the Sunday envelope by dropping it in the offering on Sunday or in the mail during the week (self-addressed, postage paid).

2. Give online anytime at www.journeymetro.com/giving.

3. Use your bank's website to arrange for a check to be sent automatically to The Journey on your timetable (most banks offer this service for free).

4. Learn more about the automated bank debit option—our most convenient way of giving. Simply reply to this email for more information about getting started.

Over the last few months we have seen God working in our church, and you have a part in what he is doing. Our church is supported by its regular givers.

Thanks for investing in eternity!

Pastor Nelson

P.S. For more on what God says about giving and stewardship, check out this article on our website: www.journeymetro.com/resources/godandmoney.

For a downloadable version, see www.MaximizeBook.com.

link to an article on giving or other information to encourage the giver to continue educating herself. Again, at this stage, the goal is to move the new giver to regular giving.

Step 2 is to send every first-time giver a thank-you packet by Thursday of each week. The thank-you packet includes five things:

1. thank-you letter (see fig. 5 on page 101)
2. free gift—CD of a recent message on finances or a small book on finances
3. auto-debit enrollment form
4. giving envelope
5. postcard promoting the current teaching series

The thank-you packet accomplishes many goals. Primarily, it again acknowledges, thanks, and educates. The letter allows you to establish integrity by mentioning the high standards of your system, as you'll see in figure 5. The packet also provides the giver with tools for future giving. We always include an auto-debit enrollment form, but we don't mention it or explain the benefits. The form is just there as a subtle piece of information. Some people jump on it. For others, it is a seed.

You can be bold with the thank-you packet because the giver has been bold in deciding to give. He wants to hear from you and to be supported with information that undergirds his decision. He doesn't want to feel like he has given into a void. Even if the new giver doesn't fully realize it himself, he is waiting for you to come alongside him and say, "Hey, we see you. You took a great step. Thanks. You can trust us. Let's move ahead together." Don't shy away from that responsibility.

Giving people something for free goes a long way. In the past, we have included a CD of a recent message on finances in our follow-up packet. Currently, we're including my book *The Generosity Ladder*, which is a great tool for new givers. (For more information about *The Generosity Ladder*, see www.generosityladder.com.) You can decide what type of free gift will work best in your culture. Just make sure you include some kind of unexpected gift that doubles as an educational tool. This sign of generosity and investment tells new givers a lot about you and your view of stewardship. The ultimate benefit for your church far outweighs the small cost.

Including a free gift comes with another added bonus. As the marketing pros know, the gift will demand a larger envelope and make your packet look bulky, which greatly increases the chances that new givers will open it and go through the information. When it shows up in their mailbox, they'll be curious to see what's inside. If you simply send information in a thin standard envelope, they will likely toss it aside with the junk mail and never open it. Your follow-up packet won't be much good to new givers if it ends up in a pile with the other bland mail that inundates them. Make your material stand out. It is critical to a new giver's continued spiritual growth.

Liz pulls into the driveway in a rush. Softball practice ran longer than usual. It's already 6:30, and she still needs to make dinner and help her kids do their homework. As she and the kids jump out of the car, Liz notices Jon is already home. The threesome bursts through the door.

"Hey, Hon! We're home!" Liz shouts as she closes the door behind them.

"In the kitchen," Jon calls.

Liz follows the kids down the hall toward the kitchen. Madison and Johnny are already talking all over each other trying to tell Jon about their day. Liz gets to the kitchen and notices Jon must have walked in just before them. He has his tie in one hand and a stack of mail in the other.

"Looks like you just beat us. Good day?" Liz asks.

"Yeah, great day," Jon answers as he begins flipping through the mail.

"What's that big envelope?" Liz asks as she begins pulling the makings of dinner from the fridge. "You guys go ahead and start your homework," she says over her shoulder to the kids.

"I'm not sure. Oh, it looks like it's from church," says Jon. He tosses the other mail to the side and turns the bulky six-by-nine envelope over in his hands. Liz walks over to him as he tears open the envelope.

"It's a thank-you letter for giving on Sunday. Wow. Look at all this stuff. Did I tell you I got an email earlier this week thanking us?"

"They are really on it," Liz says with a smile. Jon had been hesitant to give to the church for the first time, but they both knew they needed to give. Pastor Tim had talked about it in membership class, and Liz had been feeling even more strongly about it since their baptisms. But Jon had struggled with the issue. He understood that giving would help him grow, but he still had a lot of questions, and money was tight. Finally, he had decided to take the step of faith. Liz had been thrilled when Jon picked up the offering envelope and started filling it out last Sunday. And now, she couldn't be happier that the church was being so sincere and professional in supporting the decision. She knows this will make things a lot easier for Jon next time.

"What's that?" Liz asks as she motions to the CD in Jon's hand.

"Looks like it's a message Pastor Tim did called 'Handling Your Finances God's Way,'" Jon reads off the label. "Huh. I'll load this into my iPod and listen to it while I run in the morning."

Liz turns on the stove and starts chopping some zucchini while Jon shuffles through the information in his hand.

"Hey, listen to this story. 'I struggled in my relationship with God for five years before I found . . .'" Jon continues to read the thank-you letter aloud to Liz. She tosses the veggies in the pan and wipes off her hands. While she continues to listen, she picks up and starts scanning the auto-debit enrollment form.

***

Ongoing Follow-up

Initial follow-up is only half of the follow-up equation. Once someone has given for the first time and you have completed your initial follow-up, that person is officially in your stewardship system. To make sure he doesn't get lost in the shuffle, an ongoing follow-up process needs to be in place—one that will guarantee you are connecting with him on a regular basis. Think about it this way: when someone in your church gives his life to Christ, you establish a plan for keeping in contact with him to make sure he is growing and maturing. You encourage him to take the step of baptism; you work to connect him with a small group. You don't leave him to languish and figure things out on his own. In the same way, when someone gives for the first time, we need to continue following up with him in a way that ensures his continued growth and maturity. That's part of our responsibility as shepherds.

We will dissect the details of ongoing follow-up in parts 3 and 4. For now, let me sketch the broad structure for you. Ongoing follow-up should consist of three communication checkpoints:

1. *Quarterly giving statements*: send quarterly giving statements by the 15th of the month following each quarter's end. The giving statements should be packaged much like the original thank-you packet, including a letter, a giving statement, an auto-debit enrollment form, a series postcard, and a business-reply giving envelope.

2. *End-of-year giving statement*: send every giver an annual giving statement by January 31, as required by law. This end-of-the-year statement is really the fourth of your quarterly giving statements and should be packaged in the same way.

FIGURE 5

Dear [first-time giver],

According to our records, this may very well have been your first gift to The Journey Church, and we want to thank you for honoring God with your finances by giving. We also want to take the time to express to you our commitment to financial management at this church.

At The Journey, we do all we can to maintain the highest levels of integrity with the resources God gives us through the tithes and offerings of people like you. Examples of steps we've taken include establishing policies for secure handling and counting of weekly offerings, quarterly giving statements that show your year-to-date giving, preparing an annual budget, and conducting strenuous annual accounting reviews of our financial records and controls.

Your contributions go directly to funding the ministry initiatives of our church, which affect the lives of thousands of people each week. Through your faithfulness, you are assisting us in fulfilling our mission of giving people the best opportunity to become fully developing followers of Jesus. One gentleman recently said this:

> I struggled in my relationship with God for five years before I found The Journey. I can't express how relevant the messages have been to my life. Every Sunday, I leave knowing God used the time to clear the fog that surrounded me for so long. I see more about who God is and feel closer to him.

We are grateful for your financial support of The Journey and are encouraged by your confidence in our ministry. May God bless you!

Sincerely,

Nelson Searcy

Lead Pastor, The Journey Church

Enclosures

P.S. If you have questions at any time about your giving, please don't hesitate to contact me.

For a downloadable version, see www.MaximizeBook.com.

3. *Special follow-up for unusually large gifts*: send a handwritten thank-you note, along with a copy of *The Generosity Ladder* or another applicable book of your choice, within forty-eight hours after receiving the large gift.

The thankfulness you show to your people as they give reflects the heart of your thankfulness to God for supplying the means to continue growing his church. How thankful are you? Remember what your mother taught you all those years ago. Whether you knew it then or not, she was on to something. In 1 Thessalonians 5:18, Paul tells us the same thing: "In everything give thanks; for this is God's will for you in Christ Jesus" (NASB). A simple thank-you is really quite revolutionary.

Implementing the Maximize system was huge for Canyon Creek Church. By just making some simple adjustments, our giving has increased 15 percent overnight.

Brandon Beals, Lead Pastor
Canyon Creek Church, Mill Creek, Washington
Coaching Network Alumnus

systematic givers

Teaching People to Give When They Are Paid

7

options are not optional

Providing Various Ways for People to Give

It's easy to make good decisions when there are no bad options.

Robert Half

The servant who received the five bags of silver began to invest the money and earned five more. The servant with two bags of silver also went to work and earned two more. But the servant who received the one bag of silver dug a hole in the ground and hid the master's money.

Jesus (Matt. 25:16–18 NLT)

How wise are you with your investments? Have you ever studied investing or met with a financial advisor? Even if you have very little investment experience, I bet you know the number-one rule every advisor would tell you to adhere to when managing your resources: diversification. Never put all your eggs in one basket, to quote the old cliché. When we diversify wisely, we see greater returns on our resources than when we pursue only one or two investment avenues.

The Principle of Diversification

Our wisest advisor—Jesus himself—teaches us the principle of diversification in Matthew 25. The parable of the talents tells the story of a wealthy man preparing to go on a long trip. Before he leaves, he calls his servants together and distributes his money among them. He gives five bags of silver to one servant, two bags to another, and one bag to the third. Note that this keen man does not hand over all of his wealth to one servant; he distributes it, albeit unevenly, among the three. After spreading around his resources, our traveler sets out on his journey.

The most thoughtful of the three servants decides to diversify the five bags of silver he has been given. Like his master, he understands there is security in diversity. He does not place all of the wealth entrusted to him in one place; he spreads it out among several avenues and, as a result, doubles his return. This faithful servant earns five more bags of silver. The servant who was given two bags of silver puts a couple of options to work for him and reaps some reward. He earns two more bags of silver.

Then there's the servant who has been given only one bag of his master's treasure. I think we can safely assume that, because of his perceived limited resources, he has a scarcity mentality. Fully aware he hasn't been given as much as his fellow servants, he is scared of losing the little he has. He does not understand how diversifying his options might help him, so he decides to play it safe and hold on tightly to his one bag of silver. He digs a hole in the dirt and buries the bag . . . then eats a quarter of a donut as a snack.

When the master returns from his journey, he calls a meeting to find out how well his servants handled his resources in his absence. Upon hearing the reports from the first two servants, the master is full of praise for the way they increased his profits. But things turn ugly as the fearful, hoarding servant steps forward to give his report. When the master hears that the third servant hid the treasure and failed to increase its value, the master lashes out, "You wicked and lazy servant!" (Matt. 25:26 NLT). Then he does something that seems a little extreme. He orders that the one bag of silver be taken from the lazy servant and given to the servant who best understands proper investment principles. Then he casts the unwise servant out of the kingdom. Matthew tells it this way:

> Then he ordered, "Take the money from this servant, and give it to the one with the ten bags of silver. To those who use well what they are given, even more will be given, and they will have an abundance. But from those who do nothing, even what little they have will be taken away. Now throw this useless servant into outer darkness, where there will be weeping and gnashing of teeth."
>
> Matthew 25:28–30 NLT

What does this parable have to do with the Maximize system? Everything. Let's look at the application: God is the master, and we, as church leaders, are his servants. The bags of silver he has given us are the resources he has provided for his kingdom through each of our individual churches—not just the resources you and I already bring in but the entire pool of resources available to each of us for God's work. That means a minimum of 10 percent of the combined income of every regular member and attender.

There is security in diversity.

The size of that number varies per church—some of us have been given five bags of silver, some two, and some one. What we've been given isn't the important part; how we maximize what we've been given is.

Like the wise steward in Jesus's parable knew, the best way to increase the resources entrusted to us is to diversify. The unwise servant thought he was being safe—or finding security—by holding on tightly to the little bit he had been given. Fear of losing what he had kept him from exploring avenues for increase. But as the wise servant showed us, when we explore options for increasing what the master has entrusted to us, we will reap the reward and be found faithful.

Systematic Giving

Our job is to disciple people along the path to financial stewardship. If we provide them with only one or two options for giving, we stunt their growth. We are crossing our fingers and hoping we will see some treasure, and when we do, we are burying it. We are shooting our own stewardship system in the foot. If we diversify our plan for receiving the kingdom resources God has put in the bank accounts of our regular attenders and members, we open up ourselves and our church to growth and blessing. The wisest way to diversify is to provide people with systematic giving options.

Think about this: if one of your members misses church because she is sick, does this mean she should stop reading her Bible and praying for the rest of the week? Of course not. Even if she isn't in church on Sunday, you want her to stay strong in her spiritual disciplines. I bet you even have a way for her to listen to the sermon or watch it online. But do you have a way for her to honor God through her giving if she's not in church? Or does she just have to remember to double her gift next week, when she might forget her checkbook thanks to the cold medicine? If the only opportunity people have to give is when they show up at your church on Sunday, you are crippling their spiritual development and robbing God of the resources he has provided for his work.

Once someone gives a first-time gift, your new goal is to move them to regular, or systematic, giving. A regular giver, as the term implies, is simply someone who gives on a regular basis. They give once a week, once a month, every two weeks, or whenever they are paid. The gift is not yet a tithe, necessarily, in that it is not a tenth of their income, but it is consistent. One of the most effective ways to make it easy for people to become systematic givers is to provide them with various practical options for giving. Such options allow them to remain faithful in honoring God with their finances no matter what else is going on in their lives.

I'm going to let you in on a little secret. I am not always faithful. None of us is. Sometimes I am inconsistent. Every once in a while I sleep late and don't have time for my morning devotional. Sometimes I get so busy that I neglect to reach out to unbelieving acquaintances and others in my community. There are times when my prayer life isn't as strong as it should be. But because I don't have to remember to bring my gift to church with me every Sunday, I can be consistently faithful in my giving. A system is in place that makes it easy for me—and my people—to be strong, steady stewards. And if I am obedient in my giving, then my heart is going to be continually turned toward God and his work, which is going to drive me deeper in the other areas of spiritual discipline. Providing people with options for giving is great for your budget, yes, but it is also stewardship development at its best.

At The Journey, we strive to diversify, and therefore grow, the resources God has made available to us by providing people with five options for giving:

1. Sunday service giving
2. mailed-in giving
3. online giving
4. credit/debit card giving
5. automatic bank debit giving (our preferred way of giving, as you'll see)

Let's look at each of these options in detail.

Sunday Service Giving

Sunday service giving is the best option for new givers. As I mentioned earlier, you will receive the majority of first-time gifts at the service. New givers like to use an offering envelope and drop their gift in the bucket. Since they are not yet part of the stewardship system, they probably don't even know about the four other giving options available to them. Once you receive an identifiable, first-time gift, it's time to begin moving a first-time giver toward systematic giving.

Mailed-In Giving

There are three types of mailed-in giving. The first is when someone takes the offering envelope from the bulletin on Sunday and mails it to your church later in the week. Remember how Pastor Tim told his congregation they could take the offering envelope home and drop it in the mail if they weren't ready to give at the service? There's power in providing that option. Perhaps a new giver really wants to give but didn't come prepared. Thanks to a postage-paid offering envelope, he will be able to walk out with something in his hand that will not only remind him of his desire to give but also provide an easy way for him to get his gift to you.

Since today's generation has moved so far away from traditional stamped mail, we provide postage-paid offering envelopes at The Journey. Having to find and put a stamp on an envelope may seem like a small thing, but it can be a stumbling block to a new giver trying to send in his gift. Postage-paid envelopes keep things simple and eliminate a potential excuse for not giving. The effort and cost to you are minimal.

Getting postage-paid envelopes is as easy as going online to the United States Postal Service or going to your local post office and opening an account. You deposit a small amount of money into a reserve, and every time an envelope is mailed in connection with your account, the cost is deducted from the money you've put in. You are not charged for the envelopes that don't get mailed. In my experience, we end up paying about $1 for each envelope mailed to us—the cost of the stamp plus a small processing fee. Our average mail-in gift is over $250, so I'd say $1 is well worth it. This mail-in extension of your Sunday service giving makes things easy for first-time givers or for anyone who isn't yet using an automated option.

We didn't always use postage-paid envelopes. I didn't consider them important until one Sunday when I was standing in the back of our auditorium after a service. A gentleman I didn't recognize walked up to me and pulled a wrinkled, worn offering envelope out of his pocket. He said, "I've been meaning to get this to you for the last couple of weeks, but I keep forgetting. I don't want to leave here with it again today." On a side note, I don't take checks directly, so I walked him over to one of our volunteers and asked her to make sure the envelope was placed in the offering. After our interaction, I started thinking about how carrying around one check had kept this forgetful man from writing another. If he had been able to drop the envelope in the mail as soon as he decided to give, he probably would have given a couple of times since. By not offering postage-paid envelopes, I had allowed a barrier to his stewardship. Yes, he was forgetful. Yes, he could have dropped it in the offering bucket or put a stamp on it himself. But he didn't. And since I hadn't made the effort to remove all possible obstacles, his gift—and his growth—had been delayed. Since then, we've been using postage-paid envelopes. For a downloadable version of our offering envelope and a list of recommended printers, see www.MaximizeBook.com.

The second mailed-in giving option is closely connected to the first, as it also involves postage-paid envelopes. At The Journey, we use a monthly envelope service. Once a month, the service mails a pack of four or five envelopes (depending on the length of the month) to our members. These postage-paid envelopes have our members' names printed on them, and they are addressed to our church and dated, one for each week of the month. Our members just have to drop their gift in the envelope and the envelope in the mail. Or, if they would rather, they can bring the envelope to church with them and put it in the offering bucket.

When I discovered how minimal the cost is when compared to the advantages of such a service, I decided to give it a try. The envelopes serve as a great reminder for people to give. They are essentially a little knock on the door saying, "Hey, don't forget to be faithful in your stewardship." And again, they make things easy. People don't have to fill out anything or buy a stamp. The work has already been done for them. They are free to focus on their gift. Setting up a monthly envelope service is simple. Just send your member database to the envelope company (see www.MaximizeBook.com for the service I recommend), and they will take care of the rest.

You even have the option of including a postcard or a short letter with the monthly packet.

The third option for mailed-in giving involves a bank's automatic bill pay option. Many people already use automatic bill pay for their regular monthly bills. What they may not realize is that they can also use it to regulate their giving. They just have to go to their bank's website and set up their church as a payee. The bank will cut a check for the predetermined amount and mail it to the church on the date the giver chooses. People can use this option for a one-time gift or for recurring gifts. All the while, givers don't have to touch a checkbook, an envelope, or a stamp.

Online Giving

Our culture has, inarguably, moved into the virtual realm. I know people who wouldn't know how to look up a telephone number, buy a movie ticket, or book a hotel room if they didn't have internet access. In New York, we even buy our groceries online. You go to a website, click on the grocery items you need, and within twenty-four hours your groceries arrive at your door. The power of the internet has given most of us the ability to access anything we need at any time of the day from anywhere in the world. From kids to grandparents, people are online creatures. That's why it is imperative to provide them with an online way to honor God with their giving. Just as Paul made use of the culture and technology of his day to proliferate the truth of the gospel, so should we.

Online giving allows you to establish a process for people to give automatically, which can lead to consistency. From your website, anyone who so desires should be able to set up a one-time or a recurring gift. Most church software/database management packages include an online giving element that is integrated with your giving data and easy to set up. (For more on the database system we use, visit www.MaximizeBook. com.) Once you have the process for online giving in place, make sure your people know how to access and use this option. You also need to avoid two common mistakes.

MISTAKE 1: THE ONLINE GIVING OPTION IS DIFFICULT TO LOCATE ON THE CHURCH'S WEBSITE

I am a proponent of placing your online giving option in a prominent place on your home page. Take a look at The Journey's home page (fig. 6). Notice that the online giving link appears in the main banner at the top of the page. Also, the bottom third of the page contains three large buttons: one to offer a free gift to first-time visitors of the site, one for online giving, and one for growth group sign-ups. The general online giving button may be replaced with a special giving button during the Christmas offering or a special giving campaign, but the majority of the time it stays put.

Plenty of church leaders and consultants would argue against placing a giving button on your main page, since a large portion of your web traffic is made up of people who are considering attending your church for the first or second time. They are afraid that online giving will turn off newcomers. This kind of thinking is a throwback to the improper view of stewardship discussed earlier. Contrary to their belief, a well-placed online giving option on your website is crucial to your stewardship system. Again, stewardship is part of discipleship

FIGURE 6

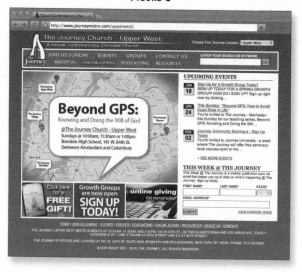

and should not be hidden. I have never met a single person who said, "Oh, I was going to visit that church, but I went to the website and saw an online giving option, so I thought better of it." Such a fear is not even logical; it's simply another skewed way for the enemy to keep giving in the dark.

MISTAKE 2: THE ONLINE GIVING OPTION IS COMPLICATED

Once people find your online giving option, the actual process for giving needs to be clear. If new givers start working through the steps of online giving and things get confusing, they will give up. People won't engage in what they don't understand. When a user clicks on The Journey's online giving button, he sees the screen in figure 7.

Here viewers read a brief explanation of online giving and a description of the two ways to give online. One is automated bank debit, which we will discuss momentarily, and the other

FIGURE 7

is straightforward online giving. Note the bottom section of the page, which says, "3 Simple Steps to Give Online Today." We want to break the process down into small segments, so there is no ambiguity. Again, remove all potential stumbling blocks. When the giver clicks on the "give online" button, our church database management system opens, guides him through the rest of the process, and automatically sends him a confirmation email when the gift is received. This is easy to set up through an online merchant account or through your existing church database management system, which most likely already offers this service.

Credit/Debit Card Giving

Credit/debit card giving is an option for people who want to use a card to make a one-time gift. If you look at our

offering envelope (see the downloadable version at www.
MaximizeBook.com), you will see an area on the inside, toward the bottom, where people can enter their credit/debit
card information. When we first added this option to our
offering envelopes, I was not convinced people would use
it. I was wrong. People use this option all the time. This is
also another area where bigger envelopes mean more money.
Make sure people have plenty of space to fill in their card
information. If their writing gets crowded or messy, they are
likely to scrap the whole thing. On a side note, our offering
envelopes contain a statement discouraging the irresponsible
use of credit cards (e.g., running up a debt). We prefer that
people use this option to give by debit.

Before offering the credit/debit card giving option, you
will need to create a merchant account with your bank
or independent provider. (See www.MaximizeBook.com
for the one we use.) Once your account is set up, let your
people know about the four ways they can give by credit
or debit:

1. They can use the offering envelope, as mentioned.

2. They can buy something at the resource table and indicate that they'd like to use the same credit card for a
   gift.

3. They can use their credit/debit card as part of the standard online giving system.

4. They can call the office and give their card number over
   the phone, and you can make the deposit directly.

Automatic Bank Debit Giving

Automatic bank debit (or auto-debit) is an automatic draft from a checking or savings account. At The Journey, we try to move givers toward auto-debit as quickly as possible after their first gift. We feel it is the most stable, most consistent, and most God-honoring way to give. Not to mention, auto-debit gives us valuable information as we make plans concerning our spending. So we are in a continual process of nudging people to sign up for this option. Remember the auto-debit enrollment form Jon and Liz received in the mail with their thank-you packet? This was an initial, subtle push toward auto-debit. Similarly, when someone decides to give online, we immediately present auto-debit as an online giving option, as you can see in the middle of figure 8.

We try to move people toward automating their giving by educating them on the benefits. First of all, automation helps givers honor God consistently with their finances. Second, auto-debit giving is simply more convenient. Once it is set up, you don't have to remember to give. Your recurring gift is automatic. Third, auto-debit gifts do not entail the same fees as standard online giving; thus, the amount that actually goes to the church increases. Now, my thinking on fees in general is that they are insignificant when compared to the value of creating new and consistent givers. Not to mention, they pale in comparison to the extra time it would take to process those same gifts offline. Still, if you can minimize the fees, why not? When we clearly communicate these three reasons to automate—you are honoring God, it's convenient, and more of your money goes where you want it to go—we see high auto-debit enrollment numbers.

Auto-debit is a giving option you can set up with your bank, just like businesses do. That's actually how God pointed me toward this idea. One day, I started thinking, "If the power company can tap into my bank account to cover my bill automatically every month, why can't my people give to the church in the same way? Why should they have to remember to write a check and bring it to church? If the gym can take a set amount of money from my account every month, why can't we set up the same thing for those who want to automate their giving?" Thankfully, the bank we work with was able to set up this kind of auto-debit with no problem. Check with your current bank first, but if they don't have an auto-debit option, contact other banks in your area.

To get started with automated giving, a giver needs to fill out the auto-debit enrollment form and turn it in to your church's office. They can do this by printing the form from your website and faxing or mailing it in. Or they can send in a form they receive in the program or thank-you packet. On the form, they indicate their bank routing information, the amount they want to give, and with what frequency. Whenever they need to change the amount or the frequency, they can just call the church office and you can log on to the system and make the changes. Your givers don't have to log in anywhere or remember a password. They sign up, and you take it from there.

Over the years we have tweaked our auto-debit enrollment form for better results. The form we use now looks professional—more like something you would expect to fill out at a bank rather than a church—which gives people a feeling of security. There is an inside and an outside, so if people drop this form in the offering bucket, they don't have to worry about their personal information being exposed (see fig. 8).

Thanks to the automated giving option, we are never caught off guard by an unexpected dip in attendance. We could have six blizzards in a row, and our giving would remain amazingly consistent. I can tell you at any given time how much money we will receive on the first and the fifteenth of the upcoming month, which allows us to plan and prepare for ministry more effectively. And the faithfulness of our stewards who have decided to automate is rewarded tenfold. These givers can go on a summer vacation and not miss an opportunity to worship God through giving. They can deal with an illness or an unexpected expense and not feel the temptation to draw from the money they are giving back to God. Regardless of life's fluctuating circumstances, our givers' hearts are faithfully tied to God's work because their treasures are faithfully entering his kingdom.

As part of our goal to move all givers toward auto-debit, we keep a close watch on how people give and continually work to help them take the step of automation. Every six months, I pull a list of people who are using the other options and send them a personal letter inviting them to switch to auto-debit. I do the same thing through email about once per quarter. I want to take every possible opportunity to remind people of an easier way to give.

You won't get everyone to automate. That's why four other options are available for systematic giving. Diversification

Figure 8

The Journey
AUTOMATED GIVING Enrollment Form

There are two ways to automate your giving at The Journey:
- Have your gift automatically deducted from your bank account.
- Have your gift automatically processed on your credit card.

To enroll, complete this form and drop it
in the offering bucket, or mail to:
The Journey Church, c/o Financial Administrator
321 W. 44th St., Suite 203A, New York, NY 10036

General Information:

Name: _____

Address: _____

City: _____ State: _____ Zip: _____

Email: _____

Telephone number: _____

Select one of the following:

❑ New enrollment ❑ Change in amount* ❑ Change in account

Frequency and Amount of Transfers:

❑ 1st of every month in the amount of $ _____

❑ 15th of every month in the amount of $ _____

❑ 1st & 15th of every month in the amount of $ _____

When do you want your automated giving to begin? _____

*To change the amount of your automated gift, you can call or email the new information
to The Journey Office, or fill out and return this form. Account numbers are not neeeded
to make a change.

OPTION 1: Bank Debit (Preferred Option)
❏ **Enroll me in Automated Bank Debit**

Please make my gift payment
directly from my:

❏ Checking account

❏ Savings account

> PAY TO THE
> ORDER OF _____ $ ☐
> _____ DOLLARS 🔒
>
> Memo _____
> ⑆121140713⑈ 1355 ⑈0005588888⑈
>
> **Routing Number** | **Check** | **Account Number**

Account number: _____

Routing number: _____

OPTION 2: Debit / Credit Card
❏ **Enroll me in Automated Debit / Credit Card Giving**

(NOTE: We offer the opportunity to donate by credit card as a convenience
to those who manage their finances in a God-honoring way.)

Name on card: _____

Type of card: ❏ Visa   ❏ MasterCard   ❏ American Express

Credit card number: _____

Expiration date: _____

Billing address (if different than mailing address):

Address: _____

City: _____ State: _____ Zip: _____

Authorization:

I authorize The Journey Church to process debit entries to my account as
indicated herein. This authority will remain in effect until I give reasonable
notification to terminate this authorization.

Authorized signature: _____

All gifts are tax-deductible.

For a downloadable version, see www.MaximizeBook.com.

is key. But as much as possible, use your diversified options to move people toward automation, for the benefit of both your church and their spiritual growth. By encouraging your givers to automate, you are helping them take the next step in becoming fully developing stewards of God's resources. As you do so, you too become a wiser, more effective steward of the treasure your master has placed in your hands.

> Since implementing the principles from Maximize, we have seen our church experience revitalized enthusiasm and health in our church finances. Repeatedly we have heard our members thank us for the various methods of giving, such as the postage-paid envelopes, the online giving option, as well as automated debit. We exceeded our annual budget the last two years. We have also been able to purchase twenty-one acres of land for our future church home. As the senior pastor of Bridgeway, I am so thankful for the tools the Maximize system has given us to accomplish the mission of bringing more and more people into a life-changing relationship with Jesus Christ.
>
> Joel Eason, Senior Pastor
> Bridgeway Church, Tampa, Florida
> Coaching Network Alumnus

8

from first-time givers
to regular givers

Helping People Take the Step

I ask you to begin giving, and to continue as you began. . . .
You'll find in the end that you got far more than you ever
had, and did more good than you ever dreamed.

Stephen King

On the first day of each week, you should each put aside a
portion of the money you have earned.

Paul (1 Cor. 16:2 NLT)

An inclination to give is written on the soul of every man and
woman, no matter how muted it may be by present concerns

or lack of belief. Sometimes it takes a traumatic experience to bring that God-given pull toward generosity to the surface. Horror novelist Stephen King is not usually associated with purporting biblical truth. But in a commencement speech delivered to Vassar graduates in May of 2001, he offered some powerful insight to his audience—believers and unbelievers alike—on living an openhanded life. God often speaks through unlikely sources. In his address, this "pagan king" of our day who has penned numerous best sellers dealing with the depths of darkness, shined the light on giving with a sense of understanding that many of the Christians sitting in our churches lack. Here's an excerpt of his poignant comments:

> A couple of years ago I found out what "you can't take it with you" means. I found out while I was lying in a ditch at the side of a country road, covered with mud and blood and with the tibia of my right leg poking out the side of my jeans like a branch of a tree taken down in a thunderstorm. I had a MasterCard in my wallet, but when you're lying in a ditch with broken glass in your hair, no one accepts MasterCard.
>
> We all know that life is ephemeral, but on that particular day and in the months that followed, I got a painful but extremely valuable look at life's simple backstage truths. We come in naked and broke. We may be dressed when we go out, but we're just as broke. Warren Buffet? Going to go out broke. Bill Gates? Going out broke. Tom Hanks? Going out broke. Steve King? Broke. Not a crying dime.
>
> All the money you earn, all the stocks you buy, all the mutual funds you trade—all of that is mostly smoke and mirrors.

It's still going to be a quarter-past getting late whether you tell the time on a Timex or a Rolex. No matter how large your bank account, no matter how many credit cards you have, sooner or later things will begin to go wrong with the only three things you have that you can really call your own: your body, your spirit, and your mind.

So I want you to consider making your life one long gift to others. And why not? All you have is on loan, anyway. All that lasts is what you pass on. . . .

We have the power to help, the power to change. And why should we refuse? Because we're going to take it with us? Please. Giving is a way of taking the focus off the money we make and putting it back where it belongs—on the lives we lead, the families we raise, the communities that nurture us.

A life of giving—not just money, but time and spirit—repays. It helps us remember that we may be going out broke, but right now we're doing O.K. Right now we have the power to do great good for others and for ourselves.

So I ask you to begin giving, and to continue as you began. I think you'll find in the end that you got far more than you ever had, and did more good than you ever dreamed.[7]

I wouldn't venture to guess how familiar Mr. King is with the Old Testament, but intentionally or otherwise, his remarks on giving support perfectly the book of Ecclesiastes's observation that "we all come to the end of our lives as naked and empty-handed as on the day we were born. We can't take our riches with us" (5:15 NLT). They also echo Jesus in the New Testament: "It is more blessed to give than to receive" (Acts 20:35). Whether he realized it or not, Stephen King's words ring with biblical accuracy as they urge listeners not only to begin giving but to continue giving. In our lingo, that's called becoming a regular giver.

Helping People Become Regular Givers

Once you construct the foundation of the Maximize system through your cultivation of first-time givers, the rest of the steps in the continuum build naturally on this base. The foundation relies specifically on understanding and implementing what we have discussed so far: seeing stewardship as discipleship, creating a culture of generosity, encouraging gifts through education and strategic stewardship practices, and following up with givers effectively. When you do those things right, you lay the groundwork for moving people toward regular giving, tithing, and ultimately extravagant giving.

Creating regular givers involves mobilizing first-time givers to continue down the path of stewardship. As we've established, the first step to cultivating givers in your church is to educate them regarding the biblical basis of stewardship. To move them from a first-time gift to regular giving, you must keep educating them. Continuing education gives first-time givers the tools, resources, and understanding necessary for them to become regular givers.

Four key elements go into this continuing education. Two are important to every area of the system and have already been discussed at length, and two are more specifically targeted to this stage of disciple development. The four keys are:

teaching, challenges, small groups, and membership class. When utilized well, these four elements will move first-time givers into the discipline of regular giving.

Key 1: Teaching

Teach the biblical basis for stewardship during your worship services.

Ongoing stewardship teaching is essential to the Maximize system. It should be part of the fabric of your church. Your people should expect you to talk about biblical stewardship as often and as comfortably as you talk about prayer, Scripture study, and serving. As Paul says in Hebrews 4:12, "For the word of God is alive and powerful. It is sharper than the sharpest two-edged sword" (NLT). As you are faithful in teaching on giving four times per year, incorporating testimonies into your service, and offering resources that allow your people to continue their study (refer to our discussion in chap. 4), God will use the truth of his Word to convict people in different ways at different times.

The next time you preach on giving, consider the significance of this truth: as you speak the powerful, living Word of God, it will resonate with givers all along the stewardship spectrum, meeting them exactly where they are. Non-givers may be convicted to give. Initial givers will begin to realize the importance of regular giving. Regular givers will pick up on what you are saying about the tithe, and so on. Your job is to teach the fullness of what the Bible says about stewardship. God tells us that the living nature of his Word will graft that teaching into people's hearts as needed.

The primary verse to include in your teaching that will connect with people who need to begin giving regularly is found in 1 Corinthians. When talking to the church in Corinth, Paul instructs, "On the first day of each week, you should each put aside a portion of the money you have earned" (16:2 NLT). Paul is telling his listeners to begin giving systematically—not just when the Spirit moves them or when a little extra money comes into their household. He is saying, in essence, that people should set aside their gifts for God with predetermined regularity. In our culture, that translates to "give when you are paid." Teach your people that when God blesses them with income, the proper response is to set aside a portion of that money immediately to give back to his work. At this point, they may not give a full tenth, but at least they will learn to establish the practice of disciplined, systematic giving.

On a side note, while regular giving is a step on the stewardship continuum, I like to skip it whenever possible. If I can encourage someone to move directly from a first gift to tithing, all the better. If that giver exhibits an understanding of the command to tithe and has a heart for becoming more like Jesus, I will do my best to move him past regular giving to the level of full obedience. But most people will not begin tithing right away, so you need to have this level of the process in place. When your initial givers begin to incorporate the practice of regular giving into their lives, it's then a small step to move them to proportional obedience (more on that in part 4).

Key 2: Challenges

Utilize an annual giving challenge to motivate people to give regularly over a set period of time.

People respond to challenges. Thankfully for us, this is true at every level along the stewardship continuum. Just as issuing a challenge can spur non-givers to give for the first time, that same challenge can encourage initial givers to begin giving regularly—for a set period of time anyway. Remember that the best giving challenges utilize a timetable. Instead of challenging people to begin giving regularly from now until Jesus comes back, challenge them to take the step of giving regularly for six, eight, or twelve weeks. Here's what you'll find: when first-time givers commit to and follow through with the next step of regular giving over a set period of time, they won't want to stop when the challenge ends. They will see God working in their lives. Their hearts will be more attuned to his purposes than ever before, and they will be going deeper in their spiritual walk. Don't neglect the power of issuing a challenge; it will be life changing for those who accept it.

Liz glances around at all the people at the service. This is just the third Sunday since the kids started back to school, and it looks like everyone decided to get back to church too. The place is packed. Pastor Tim is kicking off a new series today. The church is abuzz with excitement.

During the message, Liz's mind wanders a little. She begins thinking about the thank-you packet she and Jon received in the mail a few weeks ago. They hadn't given again yet—of course, it hadn't been that long, and they were definitely planning on it. Jon just always struggled with letting go of money. But he had learned a lot from the CD on handling money God's way, and he had been making comments about giving lately. Liz knew they were close to making more of a commitment.

Almost as if on cue, Pastor Tim says something about giving. Liz snaps to attention.

"Look at the back of your connection card. I want to draw your attention to a couple of things," Pastor Tim says. "First of all, I want to challenge you to be here for the rest of this series. Will you make a commitment to join us over the next six weeks?"

Jon and Liz both check the box next to that commitment.

"Related to that, I want to challenge you in your giving. If you have never given, perhaps you need to take that step of faith and get started with an initial gift. If you have been giving sporadically, I challenge you to use the duration of this series to begin giving regularly. I challenge you to give consistently for the next six weeks. Maybe you want to give every Sunday when you attend, or maybe you want to go online and sign up to have your giving automated. We have options available to help you be faithful in this commitment."

Pastor Tim pauses and looks around the auditorium. Then he continues, "That is my challenge to you. If you are willing to accept the challenge, I can assure you that God will honor your efforts. You will grow closer to him through the process.

So if you want to take the giving challenge, just check that box on the back of your connection card. You won't regret it."

Liz looks over at Jon as he looks up from his connection card. As soon as they make eye contact, they both know it's time—time to step out in faith once again. God is calling them deeper.

Liz checks the box marked "Accept the Giving Challenge" and watches as Jon does the same. As she looks back into his eyes, she worries she might see hesitancy or fear, but the only thing she sees is peace. She offers up a quick thank-you as she finishes getting her card ready to drop in the offering bucket.

After the service, collect the names and contact information of those who accepted the giving challenge and send them an immediate note of acknowledgment. Then send them ongoing encouragement throughout the challenge. We'll discuss the details of giving challenge communication in part 4.

Key 3: Small Groups

Provide at least one stewardship small group each year and utilize your overall small-group system to emphasize the importance of regular giving.

Stewardship small groups are an opportune way to enhance your attenders' financial education. People want the truth about money and will sign up in droves. Thankfully, many stewardship small-group curriculums are available that do a great job informing and encouraging givers. (See www.

MaximizeBook.com for a list of suggested small-group studies.) When given the chance to dig into money matters in a small-group setting, people digest the information quickly and grow in their stewardship.

In fact, my experience has been that for every one hundred people who participate in a stewardship small group, overall giving increases by $100,000. In other words, just by participating in eight to twelve weeks of group study on stewardship, people step up their giving by an average of $1,000 per year. I don't know about you, but when I first discovered this increase, I wanted everyone in my church to be part of a stewardship small group. What great evidence of people getting their financial lives on track and pursuing deeper discipleship through the discipline of giving.

> *For every one hundred people who participate in a stewardship small group, overall giving increases by $100,000.*

The small-group system itself can also be used to encourage giving. At The Journey, everyone who joins a small group signs a covenant that details some basic decisions we want them to make for the duration of the group. The covenant asks people to make a strong overall commitment for a short period of time by agreeing to several smaller commitments. One of those commitments is to be active in the church through giving (see point 2 in fig. 9). Including this expectation in the covenant encourages those who have never given or who have given only sporadically to take the next step in their giving. For some that may mean giving a first gift, but for most it will mean moving toward regularity. Like the giving challenge, the small-group covenant provides people with a reason and an

FIGURE 9

The Journey Growth Group Covenant

Welcome to growth groups at The Journey. Congratulations on your desire to grow deeper in your relationship with God through this weekly study and the relationships that will begin in this growth group.

As a member of this group, you will be asked to enter into a covenant with the other members to make this growth group a priority. To be a part of the group, you are asked to make the following commitments:

1. I will make this group a priority by attending each week, keeping up with my assignments, and participating in group discussion.

2. I will regularly attend The Journey services and contribute to the ministry of the church through my attendance, giving, service, and inviting of others.

3. I will strive to build authentic relationships with those in this group by showing care, providing encouragement, and praying for their needs.

4. I will serve together with my group once a month during the semester. I will participate in at least one mission project with my group. I will participate in a fun activity with my group at least once.

5. I will explore honestly my next steps for spiritual growth.

Name _____

Date _____

For a downloadable version, visit www.MaximizeBook.com.

opportunity to give consistently for ten to twelve weeks. (For more information on The Journey's semester-based small-group system, which garners 100 percent participation every semester, see *Activate: An Entirely New Approach to Small Groups*, Regal, 2008, and the small-group resources at www.ChurchLeaderInsights.com. For a free *Activate* overview report, go to www.MaximizeBook.com.)

Your small-group system can help your stewardship system on another level. At The Journey, we identify new small-group leaders from within current groups. If someone has been committed to the church and has been a faithful, active participant in a few groups, we may contact him about being a group leader. Now, this person may not be a member yet. He may not be a consistent giver. That doesn't mean we can't call on him as a potential leader. If things work out and he agrees to be a group leader, he has to attend Growth Group Leadership Training. During the training, every leader is asked to sign a "Growth Group Leader/Coordinator Covenant," which is similar to but more in-depth than the growth group covenant above. By signing the covenant, the new leader agrees to participate in the church through financial giving (see point 2 in fig. 10).

Being a group leader is obviously a deeper commitment than being a group member, so we emphasize the higher level to which leaders are called. We challenge every leader to give at least regularly, if not move on to tithing. So when people join a group, they are encouraged to begin giving and hopefully make a commitment to give regularly for a set period of time. But when people become leaders, regular giving and the progression toward tithing is a must. To become a team leader—the next rung on our small-group leadership ladder— people need to meet the requirement of consistent tithing . . . and so the spiral continues. As an aside, if a potential leader is not yet a member, he can lead one group without going through membership class, but no more. If he hasn't started giving regularly by the end of the first group, he will be challenged again in membership class, as you'll see below.

The bottom line is you can't allow people to climb the leadership ladder without also moving up the generosity lad-

FIGURE 10

The Journey Growth Group Leader/Coordinator Covenant

Thank you for serving as a growth group leader/coordinator at The Journey. As a growth group leader/coordinator you will be viewed by those in your group as a leader in the church. As a result, we ask that you enter into covenant with the other growth group leaders/coordinators by making the following commitments:

1. I will embody and reflect the values and principles of The Journey and will follow the leadership of the staff team.

2. I will faithfully attend The Journey on Sundays and:

   - intentionally identify and greet those in my growth group.
   - participate in the church through my financial giving.
   - lead my group in serving together once a month.

3. I will make my growth group a priority by:

   - faithfully attending my growth group.
   - preparing beforehand for my group each week.
   - inviting/welcoming others to join my group.

4. I understand that I am responsible for the care of my growth group. As a result, I will:

   - pray for the individuals in my group.
   - follow up with each person in my group.
   - lead my group in providing care for one another.

5. I will strive to create an environment of growth in my group by:

   - involving as many people as possible in group discussion.
   - creating a safe, comfortable, and welcoming environment.
   - beginning and ending on time.

Name _____

Date _____

For a downloadable version, visit www.MaximizeBook.com.

der. If you do, you will eventually find people at high levels of leadership in your church whose hearts are far from God. This situation only leads to problems and pain. Avoid it by putting a system in place that continually encourages people to move deeper into stewardship.

Key 4: Membership Class

Utilize your membership class to emphasize the importance of regular giving.

Your membership class gives you an open door to challenge people to take the next step of commitment in their stewardship. I am working on the assumption that most of us, in current churches, utilize some sort of membership class to educate people on the expectations associated with membership. At The Journey, we hold a two-and-a-half-hour class every couple of months. We use the time to tell those interested in membership more about the history of our church and our vision for the future, introduce them to some key staff and leaders, and go over the membership requirements. During the class, we pass out a membership covenant that outlines our expectations for members. We thoroughly explain each point, then ask everyone to sign the covenant and return it to us as a way of signifying their commitment. Each of the points is critically important in and of itself, but for the present discussion, let's focus on the one that relates to giving expectations for a member (see fig. 11).

Agreements on the front end prevent disagreements on the back end. We let our potential members know that, just as

138

they are expected to be baptized, serve, and attend church, they are also expected to give in a God-honoring way. We don't require new members to tithe—not all of them are ready to take that step—but we do require them to give at least regularly. During the class, we provide a giving envelope and talk about the importance of giving accountable gifts. Notice that we also encourage them toward auto-debit. We provide auto-debit forms in the class and highlight some of the advantages of automated giving. About 20 percent of our new members sign up for that giving option on the spot. But whether they move to auto-debit right away or not, the key here is that they agree on the giving expectations associated with membership.

As we go over the covenant, we clearly articulate that we are going to hold them to the commitments they make. We explain that our job is to help them develop as followers of Jesus and that we would not be fulfilling our duty if we didn't encourage them to stand strong in their spiritual disciplines. As part of the covenant agreement, we let them know that if we see a problem beginning to develop in any of these areas, we will be in touch with them. If they are out of a small group for more than a couple of semesters, we are going to call them. If they aren't giving, we are going to call them. Our heart is for our people to be continually growing in their faith. We refuse to let any of the sheep we have been entrusted with slip through the cracks.

If someone turns in a membership covenant form and the box next to the giving commitment isn't checked, we have a conversation about their concerns. Usually, they just have a question or two that needs to be answered and then they

FIGURE 11

Baptism

Have you participated in adult believer's baptism by immersion? Yes ☐ No ☐

If yes, when? _____

☐ I'm interested in being baptized at The Journey:

☐ Sunday, February 22 from 3:30–4:30 at East 7th Street Baptist Church

☐ I can't make it on February 22, but send me information on the following baptism.

Serving

☐ Sign me up to serve at The Journey once a month on the Sunday listed below.

Circle the Sunday of the month:

1st Sunday   2nd Sunday   3rd Sunday   4th Sunday

Circle one of the six Sunday services:

Journey—Manhattan: 10:00 a.m., 11:30 a.m., 1:00 p.m., 6:30 p.m.

Journey—Brooklyn: 11:15 a.m.

Journey—Queens: 11:00 a.m.

I can serve at weekday opportunities.

☐ Monday ☐ Tuesday ☐ Wednesday ☐ Thursday ☐ Friday

Giving

☐ I commit to give regularly to my local church, The Journey.

☐ Contact me about giving through the auto-debit option.

Next Steps

☐ Reserve a spot for me at The Journey Kidz Overview on Sunday, February 1.

Circle one location.   Manhattan   Queens   Brooklyn

☐ I want to receive information on the South Africa Mission Trip (July 8–19).

Send me information about:

☐ Journey Kidz   ☐ Worship Arts   ☐ EPIC Groups

☐ Counting Team   ☐ Leading a Spring 2010 Growth Group

1. I will protect the unity of my church by:

   acting in love toward other members.

   refusing to gossip.

   following the leaders.

2. I will share the responsibility of my church by:

   praying for its growth.

   inviting the unchurched to attend.

   warmly welcoming those who visit.

3. I will serve the ministry of my church by:

   discovering my gifts and talents.

   being equipped to serve by my pastors.

   developing a servant's heart.

4. I will support the testimony of my church by:

   attending faithfully.

   living a godly life.

   giving regularly.

Name _____

Date _____

For a downloadable version, visit www.MaximizeBook.com.

will commit. If not, we tell them they can continue being a regular attender as long as they'd like, but they can't move into membership until they are ready to take the step of stewardship. To put this conversation in perspective, in all the years The Journey has been in existence, only three or four people who wanted to become members wouldn't commit to regular giving. Usually, by the time people get to membership class, they understand the basic importance of stewardship in their lives and in their relationships with God. They may not be tithing or giving extravagantly yet, but they are on the continuum.

Inevitably, you will have members who start out strong with their regular giving, but for some reason things begin to wane. As we discussed, giving is an indicator of what is going on in someone's heart. If you see a change in a person's giving or see that he is not giving regularly, you can be sure that something is not right in his life and/or his attitude toward God. Thanks to the fact that we are clear in our requirements up front, we have permission to talk to our members when we see this happen. Don't be afraid to have this conversation. You are simply holding people accountable to their commitments. Ninety-nine percent of the time, when I make a call related to a problem with giving, it goes something like this.

"Hey, Joe. This is Nelson from The Journey. We are doing our annual membership review, and your name showed up on my desk. Our records show that you haven't given anything this year."

"I knew you were going to call me. I've been expecting it. We have really been struggling financially, but I know we need to give, so this is a wake-up call. . . . (Or) We don't want to give anymore. We decided to stop. . . . (Or) We just didn't have the guts to tell you we've moved to another church."

When Joe gives me something along the lines of the first response, I say, "Okay, I'm glad I checked in. Let's take the next six months and try to get you back on track." If he gives me a version of the second response, I say, "What I hear from you is that you want to temporarily put your membership on hold." Then I try to get him back in a group (because the likelihood is that he isn't in one) and encourage him to get involved in the weekend service. If he gives me the third response, I simply wish him well and move on.

Even when these situations come up, they are rarely contentious thanks to the agreements made at the membership class. If you tell people you are going to keep in touch with them and are going to contact them if there's a problem, they will expect your call when things go askew. Generally, the phone call leads to a simple explanation and a solution. In those other infrequent cases, it will help you identify someone who is derailing and give you the chance to intervene.

Following Up with Regular Givers

Follow-up at this stage is subjective. My main goal is to recognize progress when I see it. For example, when someone gives over a certain amount for the first time, I send a short letter of encouragement. This is not always clean, but here's how it works. Periodically, I ask our accounting people to pull a list of everyone who has given over, say, $300. We do not follow up with the solid, regular givers who reach and exceed that amount as part of their usual giving. Such continuous follow-up would be counterproductive and, dare I say, annoying. But if some new people pop up on the list, I send them a brief letter saying, "Our financial people told me you have really stepped it up lately in your giving. I'm glad to see that because it says a lot about your heart. It says you are willing to grow and take some steps of faith. I just wanted to let you know I am here if you need anything." Simply be aware of those people who cross a certain marker for the first time, and say thank you when they do.

As you build your Maximize system, remember that money is not really about money. In *Money, Possessions, and Eternity*, Randy Alcorn says, "When we look at money only as money, and not in light of its impact on eternity, we walk away with a cloudy and shortsighted vision."[8] Money and its use are indicators of spiritual health. As you educate and challenge people to see the importance of honoring God's call to pass it on, you will be discipling them into a place of deeper intimacy with him.

Regular giving changes people. The act of systematically acknowledging God as the source of their money and returning money to him as an act of worship draws the hearts of men and women closer to his heart. They begin to see the eternal reality that money is a tool—a tool used by God to fully resource the work of his church on this earth and a tool for their continued transition into the likeness of Jesus. When they truly comprehend this reality, they can't wait to give in a God-honoring way.

> It had always been my philosophy that "if we do what God wants, he will raise up the money." I zealously refused to concentrate on stewardship as an essential part of my responsibility as a pastor. As a result, we were often hurting financially, my board was angry and losing respect for me, and many of God's people were not experiencing the joy of being faithful with the funds he had entrusted to them. We were a declining church that

was quickly becoming divided. I was on the verge of giving up in defeat.

Nelson Searcy's Maximize system was a crucial part of our turnaround. As a result of applying many of the truths and suggestions from this system, the change in our church has been immediate, significant, and lasting. God has totally changed the spiritual temperature of our church. Our church is now more united than we have ever been, and our leaders are trusting me again. As of the beginning of this ministry season, our attendance was running 10 percent ahead of what it was last year, and our giving had increased more than 30 percent. Now we are preparing to take greater steps to reach more people for Jesus by investing enthusiastically in the kingdom. I can't be more thankful!

Glenn Snyder, Senior Pastor
Clayton Baptist Church, Clayton, New Jersey
Coaching Network Alumnus

9

money matters

*Financial Management
and Quarterly Giving Statements*

Jesus Christ said more about money than about any other single thing because, when it comes to a man's real nature, money is of first importance. All through Scripture, there is an intimate correlation between the development of a man's character and how he handles his money.

Richard Halverson

But people who long to be rich fall into temptation and are trapped by many foolish and harmful desires that plunge them into ruin and destruction. For the love of money is the root of all kinds of evil. And some people, craving money, have wandered from the true faith and pierced themselves with many sorrows.

1 Timothy 6:9–10 NLT

First Timothy 6:10 is one of the most misquoted and misinterpreted verses in all of Scripture. While the verse says, "*For the love of* money is a root of all kinds of evil" (emphasis added), most lay Christians and leaders alike hack off the first four words. The popular statement has become, "Money is the root of all evil." Let me clear things up. Money is not the root of all evil. The love of money is. Money is morally neutral. It takes on the characteristics of the one who possesses it. In the hands of a wise, generous person, money becomes a tool for worship, good works, family provision, and the God-focused enjoyment of life on earth. In the hands of an unknowing and/or ungodly person, money becomes a tool of power, greed, and self-indulgence.

The majority of American Christians live in the vast middle ground that lies between these two types of money handlers. They haven't yet learned how to use their money in a God-honoring way, but it's out of ignorance rather than rebellion. Culture's voice has been much louder than the church's voice on how to view and structure their finances, so unwitting Christians have fallen into the traps of materialism and debt along with everyone else. Part of our role as leaders who are shining a light on this issue of stewardship is to teach people to handle their money biblically as part of their overall financial management. When people begin to understand that giving back to God is not an option but a command and a key element in their overall financial health, they will want to be systematic givers, at the very least. And, I contend, they will quickly move toward giving the whole tithe.

The number-one reason well-intentioned Christians say they don't give on a systematic basis is because they can't afford to do so. I argue that they can't afford not to, but I guess I'm a little extreme. I say, skip lunch so you can give to God. Do whatever it takes. If you have a choice between giving and paying the light bill, give. God—not the power company—has given you life, breath, the ability to earn, and the promise of blessing when you give. The problem is that we view life on a surface level. Our goal is usually just to survive, to get by—to keep the lights on and food on the table and the flat screen on the wall and the two cars in the driveway. But I'm getting ahead of myself.

Obviously, there is a range here. Some people truly are struggling just to cover the bare necessities of life—a condition, by the way, that shouldn't keep anyone from giving. Remember the poor, widowed woman in Mark 12. But the sad truth is that most of us can't make ends meet because we are so in debt to Visa and MasterCard. We have to make that car payment on the car we didn't necessarily need. We have to pay the mortgage on the house we bought to impress our friends. We have to pay the monthly fees for our iPhones and our four hundred television channels. So we are broke. We are in bondage. We come to the end of the month and say, "Oh, I just can't afford to give."

Let me be clear: nothing is innately wrong with any of these luxuries if we can truly afford them. I am not against having a nice house or a nice car. I like my phone, and there's nothing like a football game on an HDTV. The problem comes if I am dishonoring God and living in bondage to debt in order to maintain this kind of lifestyle. If that's the case, I am not living the life of a disciple. I am living the life of a slave, and not a slave to Christ, as I should be, but a slave to the materialism of this world. The Bible speaks to the issue of debt repeatedly. Here are just three key verses:

- Psalm 37:21 NLT: "The wicked borrow and never repay, but the godly are generous givers."
- Proverbs 22:7 NLT: "Just as the rich rule the poor, so the borrower is servant to the lender."
- Romans 13:8 NLT: "Owe nothing to anyone—except for your obligation to love one another."

Again, your job and mine is to help people see stewardship as part of overall financial management. Think about all the money that would be freed up in your church if everyone was out of credit card debt. We need to help them get there and help them learn to live within their means. We need to show them how to have margin in their finances, how to step back from the edge of the cliff. For many, this will involve a paradigm shift. Culture drills materialism into our collective subconscious. The concept of "buy now, pay later" is all this generation has ever known. But as you educate your people on God's plan for money management, you will help them discover a better way to live. They will not only be free from the pressure of living a life bound to materialism, but they will also be free to enjoy the abundant life God wants to bless them with as they honor him.

Plenty of incredible books discuss the details of handling personal finances from a biblical perspective, so I won't go into the specifics here. (See www.MaximizeBook.com for a list of my top five recommendations.) I suggest you study those, not only so you can teach and train your people but also so you can gain insight into your own financial condition. Then incorporate financial management teaching into the ongoing stewardship education you provide your people. You can do this in the following ways:

- *Teach on financial management.* As I mentioned, plan to do an entire series on stewardship every three years. During this series, spend weeks on issues such as getting out of debt, setting financial goals, and creating a budget.
- *Provide financial management resources.* Package previous financial messages you've preached and make them available at your resource table, along with books and articles on money management. Create a section on your website where you can provide financial tools such as budgeting worksheets, articles on handling money God's way, and MP3 downloads of related sermons. (For free samples of what I provide, visit www.MaximizeBook. com.)
- *Offer a stewardship small group.* As discussed in the last chapter, provide at least one small group every year for those interested in getting their financial lives under control.

Educating people regarding the biblical basis of giving and cultivating first-time givers go a long way toward tuning people's hearts to the heart of God, but getting people to give systematically means we have to acknowledge their current economic state. Stewardship happens in the context of life. As we help people become wiser in their overall financial management, we will help them break free of the chains that keep them from honoring God with their money.

Part of our responsibility is to keep people updated and informed about how their money is being spent once it enters the kingdom. We can't ask people to be wise financial managers and good stewards of their resources unless we are also good stewards of what they entrust to us. Frequent contact and clear communication are essential elements of that stewardship, which leads us to quarterly giving statements.

Quarterly Giving Statements

You are missing an invaluable opportunity to communicate with your people and to keep them growing in their giving if you are mailing only an end-of-the-year giving statement. You are making an even bigger mistake if you mail that one statement in a plain, white window envelope. My bet is that it is not even being read! Instead of thinking of a giving statement as a mundane necessity, start thinking of it as a chance to inspire your givers and move them along the stewardship continuum.

At The Journey, we mail giving statements to our givers once per quarter. That's four giving statements per year— one in April, July, October, and January. Let's look at what we include in every giving statement mailer, and then we'll discuss the differences among the four statements. Every giving statement mailer includes:

- *a letter*: in the letter, I focus on three goals. First of all, I give people an update on what's happening in the church thanks to their faithful giving. I share and celebrate the things their money has helped accomplish. To that end, I try to time the mailing of the statements strategically. For example, I always wait until after Easter to mail the first quarter statement, so I can highlight the success of that day. Second, I challenge them to remain faithful in their giving. Third, I include a P.S. (people always read the P.S. of a letter first) that encourages them to take the next step in their stewardship, whether that means using the enclosed envelope to give an immediate gift or using the auto-debit form to automate their giving.

- *a postcard*: I include a postcard to promote an upcoming series, and again, I am strategic in my timing. If it's about time for your quarterly giving statement to go out, but you just started a new series a couple weeks ago, don't send it out yet. Hold the mailing until your next series is about two weeks away. Then seize the opportunity to promote the new series and to encourage your givers to attend and to invite a friend.

- *an auto-debit enrollment form*: I like to get this form in front of people as often as possible. Always include one in your giving statement mailers. Use the P.S. in your letter to encourage people to take the step of automation.

- *a giving envelope*: I mention the envelope in the P.S. Perhaps someone receiving the mailer has gotten behind on giving and needs to get back on track. The envelope gives him an easy way to give again right away.

- *a personalized giving statement*: each quarter's statement reports on the entire year, meaning, in April the statement details what a giver gave January to March; in July, what he gave January to June; in October, what he gave January to September; and in January, what he gave for the entire previous year.

Quarterly giving statements have the potential to motivate and educate givers, but they won't do any good if no one opens them. To avoid this, never send a giving statement in a standard window envelope. Nine times out of ten, it will go directly into the trash can. Be creative in your packaging. During the first, third, and fourth quarters, we usually use a six-by-nine envelope with "teaser text" printed on the outside. For the second quarter (or midyear) giving statement, we use the old direct-marketing trick of making the package bulky. Bulky mail gets opened. Let's break all this down as we examine each giving statement in detail.

First Quarter Giving Statement

Mailing date: in April, after Easter. Try to time it two weeks before a series kickoff.

Packaging: six-by-nine envelope

Envelope teaser text: use anything that applies to the content within, connects to a current cultural conversation, and/or makes your people want to see what's inside. Make sure you choose something that will pique interest, such as "Enclosed: A Report on Your Spiritual Health."

Letter: see figure 12.

FIGURE 12

April 20—   www.journeymetro.com

Dear Journey Family,   212-730-8300

Thank you for being a part of what God is doing at The Journey this year through your financial giving to your church. Enclosed is your first quarter giving statement for 20—.

So far 20— has been an exciting time of growth and expansion for our church:

- We had over 1,700 people attend one of six Easter Sunday services (an all-time high).
- Journey–Jersey City set an attendance high.
- Journey–Brooklyn launched weekly services with 125 people on Easter.
- In just the first quarter of 20—, we had 199 first-time decisions to follow Jesus.
- There were 45 baptisms, over 70 new members, and over 1,100 in growth groups!

I know God has more blessings and challenges in store for us the rest of 20—. So as we look forward to the next few months (and the upcoming Tongue Pierced and God on Film teaching series), *let me challenge you to remain faithful in your giving to your church.*

Traditionally, the second and third quarters are the toughest financially for churches. But my prayer is that they will be a time of spiritual and financial growth in our church!

As always, it's a joy to serve with you. Will you join with me to continue to pray for our church and that God will use us to make an eternal impact for him?

On the journey together,

Pastor Kerrick Thomas

Executive/Teaching Pastor, The Journey Church

Enclosures

P.S. As you review your giving statement, take time to prayerfully consider if you have been honoring God when it comes to your financial stewardship. If you have, then keep it up and commit to remain faithful. If not, then make a commitment to get your giving back on track this month and give God first place in this area of your life (maybe by taking the step to automate your giving—see the enclosed auto-debit enrollment form).

For a downloadable version, visit www.MaximizeBook.com.

Second Quarter Giving Statement

Mailing date: mid-July. Try to time it two weeks before a series kickoff.

Packaging: bulky mail. As you'll see below, the theme of the midyear giving statement letter is always consistency. Since I want my people to be consistent, I really want to make sure this one gets opened. We try to be creative in mailing something that grabs people's attention and just has to be opened. In the past, we've created bulky packages by including things such as a pen, a tin of breath mints with The Journey's logo printed on the front (these made a great noise when you shook the package), a plastic ice-cream scoop for summer, and so on. One year, we actually sent everything in banker's envelopes. Don't be afraid to think outside the box here; make your recipients want to open the mailer to see what's inside. (For more ideas, see www.MaximizeBook.com.)

Letter: see figure 13.

Third Quarter Giving Statement

Mailing date: October. Try to time it two weeks before a series kickoff.

Packaging: six-by-nine envelope

Envelope teaser text: same idea as the first quarter teaser text discussed above. If you can use this little blurb to enter into a discussion your people are already having, all the better. During the recent economic downturn, our teaser text was, "An important economic message from your pastor." The letter inside addressed the pressures people were feeling due to economic uncertainty.

FIGURE 13

July 20—

Dear Journey Family,

In this second quarter giving update, I want to share two updates and challenge you in one area.

Update 1: since January 1 of this year, over 211 people have made first-time decisions to follow Jesus in our church. Think about that number. When was the last time you were in a room with 211 people? At a staff meeting? In your apartment building? God is doing great things through our church, and your faithful giving is part of it.

Update 2: we are on track with our 20— budget, although we are in the middle of a summer dip (don't worry, it happens every year as our summer attendance is more sporadic due to vacations and travel). Looking ahead, we see great opportunities, so your faithful giving for the rest of the year will be key to our continued impact in the metro area.

And that leads me to my big challenge of this update: consistency.

Have you been consistent in your giving so far in 20—? Look over your enclosed record of giving and ask this question: am I fully honoring God by giving in a systematic way?

Systematic giving is simply giving when you are paid. If you are not being consistent, will you make a midcourse correction? If you need to catch up, why not use the enclosed envelope and send in a "makeup tithe" and get back on track?

The best way I know to ensure consistency is through an automatic giving plan. All of The Journey staff, including myself, use such a plan.

Here are three ways you can automate your giving:

1. Good: set up automated online giving at www.journeymetro.com/giving.
2. Better: use your bank's online website to set up The Journey as an auto bill pay.
3. Best: complete and return the enclosed auto-debit enrollment form.

Thank you for your continued faithful giving to the ministries of The Journey Church. As a church, we can consistently impact lives for the sake of Jesus Christ because of your consistent giving. It's a privilege to do this with you. Please continue to pray for our church!

Your friend,

Nelson Searcy

Lead Pastor, The Journey Church

Enclosures

Note: you may want to include some information about your Christmas offering in this mailing in addition to the standard contents.

Letter: see figure 14.

FIGURE 14

October 20—

Dear Friend,

The economy is on the mind of everyone these days. It dominates the radio, television, and newspapers. My email box has been full of questions and prayer requests from those in our church who are reeling from the news of the last few weeks. And the news isn't good news. Words like *recession, depression, downturn*, and *uncertainty* dominate the discussion.

Perhaps right now you are feeling financial stress, fear of the future, or even the pain of uncertain economic times. Or maybe you are like so many and simply don't know what to think! You may be asking, "How will this affect me?" "What will this do to my job?" or "How will this affect my parents or friends?"

The truth is, none of us knows the future. But I do know that living our lives by the ups and downs of the market is a very stressful (dare I say, hopeless) way to live.

In times of great uncertainty, we have to break away from the twenty-four-hour news cycles that compete for our attention and focus on the unchanging, the eternal, and the solid truths of life.

I am not a fortune-teller or a prophet, but I am a lifelong student of Scripture. Here are four truths you can hold on to regardless of the economic news:

1. *God is in charge.*

God is still on the throne, and he is not shaken by the economic uncertainties of life (or any other uncertainties for that matter). He still offers hope to those who trust in him.

"Therefore, since we are receiving a kingdom that cannot be shaken, let us be thankful, and so worship God acceptably with reverence and awe" (Heb. 12:28).

2. *God will give you peace if you call on him.*

Turn off the anxiety-producing news reports and open the Good News of God's Word. Spend some time reading your Bible and praying each day. And remember this promise:

"Give all your worries and cares to God, for he cares about you" (1 Peter 5:7 NLT).

3. *God will give you all you need if you put him first.*

While it's tempting to take control of our finances when the future is uncertain, let me challenge you to do the opposite. Give control of your finances to God and put him first. If you do, he will give you all you need.

"[God] will give you all you need from day to day if you live for him and make the kingdom of God your primary concern" (Matt. 6:33 NLT).

4. *God will use you more in a time of crisis than in calm.*

While none of us would have wished for this time of difficulty, it is an opportunity for us, as God's people, to model to the world that our faith is not just a sunny-day faith. Throughout the ages, Christianity and God's people have had the most influence during times of crisis. Let me challenge you to model with your life and lips the four truths above and put feet to your faith by:

- being a person of generosity while everyone else is hoarding (John 3:16).
- being consistent in faith while others are fearing (2 Tim.1:7).
- showing great love and concern for your friends and inviting them to The Journey so they too can find hope (1 Peter 2:12).

I trust that these truths will be an encouragement to you!

Be encouraged,

Nelson Searcy

Lead Pastor, The Journey Church

Enclosures

P.S. On a church note, we have been very blessed so far this year, and I believe the future will be no different. God is in control! As your pastor, I can assure you that our church will not be led by the loss or gain of the Dow but by the unchanging and powerful Lord Jesus Christ. Wherever he leads we will follow.

For a downloadable version, visit www.MaximizeBook.com.

Fourth Quarter Giving Statement

Mailing date: by law, the year-end giving statement has to go out by January 15 of the following year.

Packaging: six-by-nine envelope

Envelope teaser text: the teaser text for the fourth quarter mailing is a no-brainer. Simply say, "Important tax documents enclosed." In January, everyone is on the lookout for their W-2s and charitable giving statements, so they can get things in order for their taxes. If you let them know an important tax document is enclosed, your envelope will move to the top of the pile.

Letter: see figure 15.

Ride-Along Inserts and Specific Needs

If you are familiar with the world of direct marketing, you have probably heard the term *ride-along*. A ride-along is a piece of material included in a mailing that gives people another option for consideration. In the corporate world, a company puts a ride-along into a mailer that another company is doing. For example, if I owned a custom closet company and sent out a marketing package, I could let the guy over at the clothes hanger company include a ride-along flier about his business. It's not competing with my main objective and gives the customer something else to consider.

Once a year—usually in the second quarter—we include a ride-along with our quarterly giving mailing. The piece is not from another organization, so one could argue we are stretching the term, but it does serve the intended ride-along purpose of giving the recipient another piece of relevant information

Figure 15

January 20—

Dear Friend,

Are you suffering from 20— phobia? Sure, it's a disease I just made up. But I bet you know exactly what I mean. It's the fear of what might happen this year. You know the drill by now. Crises . . . shortfalls . . . recession . . . ad infinitum.

So now we all have a choice. We can either fall away toward fear, or we can fall toward faith!

The truth is, none of us knows the future. But I do know that living our lives by the ups and downs of the market is a very stressful (dare I say, hopeless) way to live.

In times of great uncertainty, we have to break away from the twenty-four-hour news cycles that compete for our attention and focus on the unchanging, the eternal, and the solid truths of life. Here are four truths you can hold on to regardless of the economic news:

1. God is still in charge (Heb. 12:28).
2. If you call on God, he will give you peace (1 Peter 5:7).
3. God will give you all you need if you put him first (Matt. 6:33).
4. God will use your generosity even more in a time of crisis (1 Peter 2:12).

I trust these truths will be an encouragement to you!

Be encouraged,

Nelson Searcy

Lead Pastor, The Journey Church

Enclosures

P.S. Thank you for your faithful giving to The Journey in 20—. Enclosed is a record of your giving last year. And thank you in advance for your faithful giving in 20—. It's going to be a great year for our church and for the glory of God!

For a downloadable version, visit www.MaximizeBook.com.

to consider. The ride-along contains a list of specific needs people can give to—anything from a $5 book for first-time visitors to $1,000 for a laptop to $8,000 for new transportation. Many people who are slow to become regular givers and tithers will contribute to a specific need they see in black and white, especially if it is something that resonates with their heartstrings. Perhaps someone has given only one time that year to the general fund, but when he sees a computer need in the office, he's more than happy to give toward that specific need. That act of giving will prompt him a little farther down the path. (For a downloadable version of our ride-along, visit www.MaximizeBook.com.)

Once a year, mail your quarterly giving statements first class. Why? When you mail first class, the post office provides you with return addresses for people who have moved.

A seasoned church leader once told me, "Whenever you lead a church, people are going to walk up to you after the service and offer to buy things. So know what you need and how much your needs cost." He was right. Two to three times every year, people ask me how they can help out financially. They want to purchase something tangible for the church. If that's where they are in their stewardship walk, I don't want to block that gift, so I have a list of options ready. I know of things we need from the low end of the spectrum to the high end. Take that same concept and turn it into a once-a-year ride-along. The specificity will touch many people and open some fists that may still be slightly clenched.

Getting Started

If you are mailing a giving statement only once a year, let me encourage you to take steps toward doing quarterly giving statements. Jumping from one to four may be too much to take on at one time, but why not start by adding a midyear statement? Do two statements next year, then move to four the next. Make sure you take this opportunity to connect with and encourage your givers. The dividends are well worth the effort.

tithers

Challenging People to Become Proportional Givers

10

the full tithe

Obedience-Level Giving

I never would have been able to tithe the first million dollars
I ever made if I had not tithed my first salary, which was
$1.50 per week.

John D. Rockefeller

"Bring the whole tithe into the storehouse, that there may be
food in my house. Test me in this," says the LORD Almighty,
"and see if I will not throw open the floodgates of heaven
and pour out so much blessing that you will not have room
enough for it."

Malachi 3:10

If you want to start an argument in Christian circles, bring
up tithing. Few theological topics ignite the same kind of

heated discussion. Why? We've already established there is an inseparable link between a person's money and his heart. Actually, Jesus is the one who established this truth when he said, "For where your treasure is, there your heart will be also" (Matt. 6:21 NASB). So any dialogue dealing with the handling of personal finances strikes at the core of our being. As such, the differing viewpoints on giving within the Christian community are all charged by passion. No matter what side of the argument a person stands on, his checkbook stands with him, so his heart is engaged.

In broad terms, the divide over tithing comes down to a debate of legalism versus grace. Opponents contend that tithing, which has been in existence since the beginning of man (Gen. 14:20; Lev. 27:30–33) and was a command by Jewish law (Num. 18:28–29; Deut. 12:11), was abolished when Jesus came on the scene. But Scripture confirms that Jesus came to earth to fulfill the law, not to dismiss it. Jesus minces no words when he says:

> Don't misunderstand why I have come. I did not come to abolish the law of Moses or the writings of the prophets. No, I came to accomplish their purpose. I tell you the truth, until heaven and earth disappear, not even the smallest detail of God's law will disappear until its purpose is achieved. So if you ignore the least commandment and teach others to do the same, you will be called the least in the Kingdom of Heaven. But anyone who obeys God's laws and teaches them will be called great in the Kingdom of Heaven (Matt. 5:17–19 NLT).

Jesus shifted the heart of humankind from legalism to grace, but in doing so he in no way rendered the law obsolete. Consider the Sermon on the Mount. In this teaching, Jesus magnifies rather than minimizes the expectations previously associated with the law of Moses. He says, and I paraphrase, "You've heard that you shouldn't murder. Well, I say don't even be angry with anyone. You know that you shouldn't commit adultery, but guess what? Under grace, you have already done so if you even look at a woman lustfully" (see Matt. 5). The expectations Jesus places on his followers, thanks to the introduction of grace, go above and beyond the expectations of the law that preceded him. If anger is now level with murder and lust is level with adultery, doesn't it stand to reason that the tithe is now considered a base-level command—a minimum expectation now maximized through grace, like the other components of the law? Much to the contrary of being obsolete, giving under grace implies we should all be giving even more sacrificially than those who gave under the law; we should be operating at a higher level than the threshold previously mandated.

Even under the bondage of the law, devout Jews often took it upon themselves to give God more than the first 10 percent of their increase. They certainly didn't give begrudgingly. They recognized that all they had came from God, and they understood the command to return their firstfruits to him. Logic would suggest that we who have been given salvation for eternity and a purpose on this earth would also recognize the source of our blessings and feel even more inclined to return the tithe as an act of worship. We should easily recognize 10 percent as simple obedience—like we recognize not murdering and not committing adultery as simple obedience—and be filled with the desire to give at least that, if not more. Unfortunately, that's not the case.

Under grace, the average, modern-day Christian gives only 2.5 percent of his or her income, which, obviously, is nowhere close to a tithe. In *Money, Possessions, and Eternity*, Randy Alcorn writes, "When we as New Testament believers, living in a far more affluent society than ancient Israel, give only a fraction of that given by the poorest Old Testament believers, we surely must reevaluate our concept of 'grace giving.' And when you consider that we have the indwelling of the Spirit of God and they didn't, the contrast becomes even more glaring."[9] We seem to have a heart problem.

Could the problem be that, deep down, many of today's Christians who oppose the tithe do so not out of biblical study, prayer, and deduction but out of misinformation or their own sinful (perhaps even subconscious) desire to be the master of their money? Their hearts are tied to their wallets, as are all of ours, and the contents of those wallets aren't being poured into God's work. So it makes sense that their hearts—far from understanding the supernatural blessings associated with the practical funding of God's kingdom—are waging a war for financial control.

As a result, they fight against the tithe. They call tithing outdated and legalistic. Even if only subconsciously, they feel that if they can discount the biblical mandate for twenty-first-century Jesus followers to tithe, they can continue to handle their money as they please. Most of these Christians are not intentionally choosing to be selfish. They are just caught up in a problem of the heart—one that is often caused more by a lack of education about the tithe than by willful disobedience, as we will see.

Alcorn goes on to say, "The Israelites' tithes [often] amounted to 23% of their income—in contrast to the average 2.5% giving of American Christians. This statistic suggests that the law was about ten times more effective than grace! Even using 10% as a measure, the Israelites were four times more responsive to the Law of Moses than the average American Christian is to the grace of Christ."[10] Let that sink in. Do you think that's what Jesus intended when he said he didn't come to abolish the law but to accomplish it? He calls us to go deeper and higher in our pursuit of God's desires—not to use his presence as an excuse to fall beneath the bar set by the law.

Tithing opponents rely most heavily on the argument that we are free from the law; we have the liberty of giving to the God of our salvation through grace—and that is a true argument. But a piece of the puzzle they are putting together is missing. While they purport tithing as legalism, our churches are operating in lack. We are not properly resourced. We do not have enough money for missions. We cannot do the kinds of ministry we'd like to do. Our people are not growing spiritually and are awash in the cultural mind-set of consumerism. God's desire for our submission to the tithe is being massacred rather than magnified, and we are suffering the consequences. This missing puzzle piece begins to take shape with Jesus's words, "Yes, you should tithe and you shouldn't leave the more important things undone either" (Matt. 23:23 NLT). He addresses tithing as something so understood that it's almost unworthy of a mention. We are free from the law, yes. We have been called to live by the higher standard of grace.

Sometimes we just need to take a step back and examine why we believe what we do. What substantiates our positions? How do they measure up with God's reality? Maybe God was on to something when he came up with the idea of resourcing his work on this earth through the faithful tithes of his people, knowing that both they and the church would grow through the giving. Maybe that's why he made bringing the firstfruits to him a command, maximized by grace. Now if he could only get us to stop arguing out of our ignorance and get on board with the plan. This is where a proper understanding of biblical stewardship comes in. We need to educate ourselves. To bring giving into the light, we have to be willing to step out of the darkness.

Obedience-Level Giving

Let's take a look at one of the most famous giving passages in all of Scripture—Malachi 3. In verses 8–10, God, addressing the people of Israel, says:

> "Will a man rob God? Yet you rob me. But you ask, 'How do we rob you?' In tithes and offerings. You are under a curse— the whole nation of you—because you are robbing me. Bring the whole tithe into the storehouse, that there may be food in my house. Test me in this," says the LORD Almighty, "and see if I will not throw open the floodgates of heaven and pour out so much blessing that you will not have room enough for it."

In this passage, God clues us in to three important truths about the tithe. First of all, if we are not tithing, we are robbing him. Partial obedience is complete disobedience. We've discussed how to turn first-time givers into regular, though not necessarily proportional, givers. While that step is important, let me be clear: until our givers are bringing the full tithe to God, they are still operating in disobedience. That's why, as often as possible, I try to move people directly from a first gift to tithing. The bridge of regular giving is necessary for some, but if possible, it's always better to move people directly into true obedience.

Let me take this opportunity to define the tithe. A tithe literally means the first tenth. We are commanded to return one-tenth of our income to God—but not just any tenth. We are to give back the first tenth of all God blesses us with. In Proverbs 3:9–10, Scripture teaches us, "Honor the LORD with your possessions, and with the *firstfruits* of all your increase; so your barns will be filled with plenty, and your vats will overflow with new wine" (NKJV, emphasis added). Giving leftovers won't do. God wants the best of what we have to offer.

Consider the Genesis 4 account of Cain and Abel. God comes to the two brothers and asks them to bring him an offering. Abel, who is a shepherd, immediately brings the best of the firstborn lambs from his flock and sacrifices it before God. But Cain, a farmer by trade, approaches God's command with a different attitude. Genesis 4:3 tells us, "When it was time for the harvest, Cain presented some of his crops as a gift to the LORD" (NLT). While the Lord is pleased with Abel's gift, Cain's gift is not acceptable. In fact, the

Lord says to him, "You will be accepted if you do what is right. But if you refuse to do what is right, then watch out!" (Gen. 4:7 NLT). What was the difference? Abel immediately brought God the firstfruits of his increase. Cain, when he was ready, brought God *some* of his increase. What we give God, and when, is a testament to the ordering of our heart's priorities.

The second thing we can learn from Malachi 3:8–10 is that those who are not tithing are not being fully blessed by God. Scripture tells us that non-tithers are "under a curse." In other words, failing to tithe blocks God's ability to bless us to the extent he would like. No man can mock God. We cannot expect to disregard his plan for our personal growth and the church's proliferation and then expect to have his blessing on our life. But when we are in submission to God's rule and obedient to the call to tithe, he will bless us in unimaginable ways—both financially and otherwise. I have learned firsthand I would rather tithe 10 percent and live with God's supernatural blessing on the other 90 percent than have the full 100 percent in my pocket but operate without God's blessing.

One of the most frequent questions I hear about tithing is, "Should I tithe based on my gross income or my net income?" My answer is always the same: "Which amount do you want God to bless?" When you make a decision to tithe based on your net income, you are essentially putting the government in a position of priority over God. You are giving to him from what's left over after Uncle Sam takes his due. The government doesn't exercise grace. They know we can't be trusted to pay to Caesar what is Caesar's without an automatic enforcement. That's why they set up a system to get to our money first. Giving based on what they leave behind is not a tithe.

Third, Malachi 3 is the only place in all of Scripture where God says "test me" in a positive way. He is essentially saying, "Bring me the tithe and see if I don't bless you. Go ahead. Try it." His challenge here is to Christians and non-Christians alike. When we issue a tithe challenge to our people—which we'll discuss in the next chapter—we direct it at both believers and nonbelievers. Sometimes, I will go so far as to say, "Hey, if you think you don't believe in God, isn't it worth a few dollars of your income over the next few months to prove once and for all that he doesn't exist? You are staking your eternity on this, so why not? Why don't you tithe for a few months, and if you still think God doesn't exist, you can live the rest of your life without having to worry about it." God said to test him. All I do is call people to that challenge.

One time, I encountered a gentleman at The Journey who was a self-professed agnostic. Let's call him Ben. Ben happened to be visiting with a friend one fall Sunday when I laid out this tithe challenge. Ben was a little older than our average attenders and was in the midst of a successful career as an air traffic controller. After the service, Ben came over to me and said, "Okay. I'm going to test God. I want to take the challenge and dispel all of this foolishness." So he and I sat down and figured out what 10 percent of his income would be and divided that out over the next four months. He came to church a couple of times during the course of the challenge, but not regularly. His tithing, however, was like clockwork. Can you guess what happened? We baptized him the following summer.

Ben is not an exception to the rule. I have seen this scenario play out time and time again. God's promise about tithing is an if/then promise. If you honor me with your firstfruits, then I will pour out my blessing in your life. Test me. His promise crosses over into the New Testament. Remember Jesus's "yes, you should tithe" comment (Matt. 23:23 NLT) mentioned above? Paul follows that up in 2 Corinthians 8:7 with this instruction: "Since you excel in so many ways—in your faith, your gifted speakers, your knowledge, your enthusiasm, and your love for us—I want you to excel also in this gracious act of giving" (NLT). Ten percent is just the threshold. As we excel in grace, we should excel in giving.

Often people question not the amount of a proper gift but where it should go. Some Christians believe they should be able to distribute their tithe as they see fit. If they aren't happy with the way their church handles its finances, they think they should have the freedom to give their tithe to an outside organization. But Scripture teaches us that the tithe is to go to the local church—the one and only organization that is eternal. Offerings, any giving over and above the tithe, can be given outside the church, but not the tithe.

Let's look again at Malachi 3. God says to bring the whole tithe into the storehouse. Why? So "there may be food in my house." In biblical times, the storehouse referred to the temple. Today, it is the modern church. The "food" God refers to is the ministry of the temple or, as we understand it, the ongoing work of God through his church on this earth. The tithe is specifically intended to infuse the local church so that God's kingdom can continue to expand at the best possible rate. It is not up to you and me as givers to decide where to give our tithe. We are simply told to make it the firstfruits, make it proportional, and bring it to the storehouse.

What we've discussed here is by no means a comprehensive exegesis on the tithe, but it is a start. I encourage you to work through Randy Alcorn's *Money, Possessions, and Eternity* for an in-depth tour of everything the Bible has to say about tithes, offerings, and overall financial management. You may also want to study *The Blessed Life* by Robert Morris and *Money Matters in Church* by Aubrey Malphurs and Steve Stroope. You and I need to be beyond reproach in our knowledge of God's Word as it relates to finances. I challenge you to dig into God's Word and examine his truth for yourself. Once you have developed your own clear theology of giving, teach your people. Education is the only thing that will counteract the rampant stewardship ignorance in our churches and clear the path for givers to become fully developing stewards.

Teaching the Full Tithe

The third step along the stewardship continuum is to mobilize regular givers to become tithers. Creating tithers builds naturally on the foundation already laid as we cultivated first-time gifts and created regular givers. As with the other levels, continuing education is key. As part of the ongoing stewardship teaching that is a cornerstone of the Maximize system, you must educate people to bring the full tithe to God as an act of joyful worship.

Educate people to bring the full tithe to God as an act of joyful worship.

Don't shy away from presenting the full truth on tithing as biblical stewardship during your four yearly messages on finances and in the full financial series you do every three years. As you teach on tithing from the pulpit, make sure to highlight and thoroughly explain these three key truths:

1. Stewardship is a critical ingredient of discipleship.
2. God's clear command is to bring the whole tithe to the local church.
3. As givers grow in the grace of giving, the church grows in its ability to do God's work.

You can also underscore the blessing of tithing by having strong tithers give testimonies about God's faithfulness. Testimonies, as we've discussed, connect with people on an emotional level. They are the single most powerful tool for supporting your teaching.

In addition to regular weekend teaching, we use a class called Class 201: Discovering Spiritual Maturity to move people to tithing. We offer this class to those who have been through our membership class. In it we talk about creating disciplines that will lead to spiritual maturity, such as scheduling daily time to seek God through his Word, developing a strong prayer life, connecting with other believers through small groups, serving through gifts, and becoming obedient to God through giving. We detail the importance of tith-

ing and reinforce the various giving options. (Visit www.
MaximizeBook.com for our "Tithing Habit" notes and the
next-step card from Class 201.)

Bringing the full tithe to God is a heart issue in two ways.
First, it takes a submissive heart to be willing to give in a
God-honoring way. Second, and perhaps more importantly,
our people's hearts must be in the right place as they give
to God. We do not give the tithe out of legalism. There is
no legalism under grace. We give the tithe because God has
called us to and Jesus has amplified that call. But we must
make sure that, as we teach our people to give obediently, we
are teaching them to do so out of a desire to be transformed
into Christ's likeness.

In *Your Money Counts*, author Howard Dayton notes,
"The Lord set the example of giving motivated by love. 'For
God so loved the world that he gave his only begotten son'
(John 3:16). Note the sequence: because God loved, he gave."[11]
In the same way, we are to give not only because God wants
us to but also because we love. When people understand that
the heart of obedient giving is not bigger buildings and shiny
pews but love—love spawned by gratitude to the God of their
salvation; love that spurs their own maturity and carries God's
message to the world—they will be cheerful givers as they
bring their firstfruits into the storehouse.

11

the giving challenge

A Revolutionary Tool

What would happen if we accept God's gift of tithing when we accept God's gift of money? If we give off the top, we claim our place as "givers" before we admit that we are "consumers." That puts our priorities in order and establishes a framework of gratitude around the rest of our financial affairs.

Henry Morris

What sorrow awaits you teachers of religious law and you Pharisees. Hypocrites! For you are careful to tithe even the tiniest income from your herb gardens, but you ignore the more important aspects of the law—justice, mercy, and faith. You should tithe, yes, but do not neglect the more important things.

Jesus (Matt. 23:23 NLT)

Imagine what your church would look like if all your regular attenders, members, leaders, and staff tithed in a God-honoring way. How would that change things? Would you be able to do ministry more effectively? Would you be able to include more outreach in your budget for next year? Would you be free from constant financial worry and more focused on shepherding the flock God has given you? How different would your church look? I'd like you to think through this with me. Pull out a calculator, log on to Google, and fill in these blanks:

How many regular attenders and members does your church average? _____

What is the median annual household income in your area? (This is where Google comes in.) _____

Multiply the median income in your area by your average number of attenders/members. Then multiply that number by 10 percent. What do you get? _____

The number you just wrote down reflects the resources God wants to make available through your church for the work of his kingdom. It's what your budget could and would be if everyone in your church took the command to tithe seriously. I'm sure there is quite a discrepancy between this number and your current annual giving.

When I ran these numbers for The Journey, I realized that if everyone tithed (based on the average income in our city), our annual influx would increase by over 56 percent. If those who currently give over and above the tithe kept that up at the same rate, in addition to everyone else simply tithing, our budget would go up another 30 percent. That would be a significant amount of money being released for the kingdom. More money could go to missions, church planting, evangelism, our critical ministries . . . and so on. If everyone would just align themselves with the call to tithe, financial problems in the church would all but disappear. According to Randy Alcorn, "If Western Christians practiced tithing, the task of world evangelism and feeding the hungry would be within reach."[12] But as it stands now, some of us have trouble just keeping the doors open.

What's the answer? How do we make people understand the significance of bringing the whole tithe to God? First, through education, as discussed in the last chapter. Second, by challenging them to take God at his word and adopt a habit of tithing. The culture of tithing starts at the top, with the senior pastor, leaders, and staff. If you aren't tithing, you cannot expect your church to tithe. But as you honor God with your own finances, you can begin to establish a culture in which people consistently release 10 percent of their increase to be used for God's purposes. The number you wrote above is the treasure God has entrusted to you to do his work. Will you be like the wise servant and do what it takes to bring it to its full use? Or will you cling to the little bit you already have out of fear and ignorance? As a leader of Christ's church, the choice is yours.

The Challenged Church

Several years ago, I met a senior pastor named Roy. Roy led a church in upper Manhattan in an extremely poor and equally rough area of the city. Ever since its inception twenty years earlier, the church had struggled. The attendance was relatively large—a couple hundred people—but they never seemed to be able to meet their budget. Many months the church couldn't pay Roy's salary. The power company had shut them down on more than one occasion. Things were hard.

Shortly after we started The Journey in another part of town, Roy heard about some of the ways God was blessing our new, little church. He came to talk with me. During our conversation, he mentioned he was about to lead his church through a fall spiritual growth campaign. For some reason, I was prompted to help out. I told Roy that if he was serious about doing a growth campaign, I would buy the Bible study books for his congregation. So he told me how many he needed, and we worked out the details. As Roy was leaving my office, he turned back to me and said, "Thanks again for doing this, Nelson. I'm actually surprised you were willing to invest in our church since we have such different stewardship philosophies." Then he proceeded to tell me that he didn't believe tithing a full 10 percent to the local church was a biblical imperative.

I have to admit that my first instinct was to take back the check. But I knew I couldn't do that, so I decided to use the inroad I had gained to challenge him a little. I asked him if he had ever taken the time to study tithing in both Testaments and the transition between. Now, let me say, Roy is known to be quite a biblical scholar. He knows more about the Bible than 99 percent of the pastors I have ever met. But he admitted that he had never really studied the details of the call to give a full tithe to the local church. So I challenged him. I said, "I think it's a bad testimony that your church is having the power cut off and you can't pay your people's salaries. I know your attenders are struggling, but I believe God would bless your church if you honored him by teaching proper tithing." He agreed to take my challenge and spend some time educating himself on the tithe.

Roy's study led him to a place of repentance. A few months later, he actually stood before his congregation and repented for the fact that he had never led them into a biblical understanding of

The number-one reason most churches fail to raise biblical stewards is because the pastor is not modeling biblical stewardship.

the tithe, much less held them accountable as God had called him to do. He repented for stunting their growth as disciples. That morning Roy said to his congregation with complete confidence, "It is God's will for every one of us to return the first 10 percent of our gross income to him through our local church." Then Roy and his staff began to change everything from the top down. The leaders began tithing. They challenged the congregation to begin tithing. For the first time in the church's history, they met their budget at the end of the year—and they remained on solid financial ground throughout Roy's tenure.

One of Roy's wisest moves was to accept the call to tithe himself and to challenge his top people to tithe before challenging his congregation to follow suit. Creating a culture of biblical stewardship within your church starts at the top and works its way down, as follows:

Step 1: senior pastor begins tithing. If you are the senior pastor and you are not a consistent tither, you need to get started right away. The number one reason most churches fail to raise biblical stewards is because the pastor is not modeling biblical stewardship. As Jesus says in Luke 16:11, "If you are untrustworthy about worldly wealth, who will trust you with the true riches of heaven?" (NLT). Let me encourage you to make a few critical decisions:

- Decide to become a theological expert on stewardship.
- Decide to get your family's finances under control.

FIGURE 16

The Journey Staff Stewardship Agreement

Members of The Journey staff are expected to honor God in every area of their life—including their finances. As such, each staff person is asked to enter into a "Stewardship Agreement" that exhibits a commitment to live by biblical, God-honoring standards in the area of money and personal finances.

1. Proportionate giving. Recognizing that the tithe (returning to the local church the first 10 percent of what God has blessed you with financially) is an eternal biblical principle taught in both the Old and New Testaments, Journey staff will, at a minimum, tithe 10 percent of their gross income to The Journey Church. It is understood that the tithe is the minimal and the beginning point of God-honoring stewardship. As a staff person grows and matures in their faith, it is the church's hope that they will grow in this area and stretch themselves financially beyond just the minimal 10 percent (1 Cor. 16:2).

2. A controlled, debt-free lifestyle. Because Jesus taught that where a person's treasure is spent, their heart will soon follow, and because the way a person manages their personal finances reflects on the condition of their heart and their spiritual life, Journey staff will strive to live a financially controlled lifestyle that is free from materialism and not married to possessions. This means that staff will do everything possible to avoid unnecessary, unsecured debt and will strive to pay off existing debt in a timely fashion.

- Decide to get out of debt. (Go to www.MaximizeBook. com for a free resource on getting out of debt called "Debt-Free Pastor.")
- Decide to hold yourself and your staff accountable to bringing the whole tithe.
- Decide to make annual progress toward becoming an extravagant giver.

Step 2: hold your staff accountable for tithing. At The Journey, systematic tithing is simply a requirement of being on our staff. All staff members sign a document (see fig. 16)

3. Integrity and thanksgiving in tax payment. While no Journey staff should pay more to the government than necessary, each person should pay their city, state, and federal taxes in an honest and timely fashion. In doing so, staff members should be thankful to God that they have enough income to give back to the country that provides the freedom and opportunity that makes this ministry possible.

4. Joint financial goals with spouse. Married staff members should, in cooperation with their spouse, set wise and godly financial goals for their family. Such goals could include paying off debt, saving for retirement, investing in the future of children, living within financial means, saving for short-term goals, creating an emergency fund, etc.

5. Financial accountability. Because becoming financially stable and planning for your financial future can be difficult and confusing, it's important to have an expert outside advisor help you and your spouse plan for your financial future. For instance, 80 percent of women will one day be a widow. Outside financial accountability and guidance can help prepare you and your family for the future and assist you in meeting the financial goals you have set.

I certify that the above statement was explained to me, and I fully understand and agree.

Name _____

Date _____

For a downloadable version, go to www.MaximizeBook.com.

saying they agree to be proportionate givers. We also make sure they understand the tithe is the minimum, and we will expect them to continue stretching themselves in the grace of giving. If their giving slacks off for any reason, I don't let it slide. I have a conversation with them about it and get them back on track. When biblical stewardship becomes part of your culture, this accountability is as natural as keeping your staff accountable for spending time in the Word, spending time in prayer, and investing in relationships with unbelievers.

If we are not meeting budget, the first thing we do is look at staff giving. About half the time, simply addressing problems with staff giving gets everything back on track. The budget may be down several thousand dollars overall, while staff giving is down only a few hundred. But that dip in consistency among the staff is sin in the camp. If you and your staff aren't beyond reproach in tithing, you are blocking God's blessing on your church. As a result, problems will develop with the rest of your givers. Hold your staff accountable to the biblical model of giving and then empower and challenge them to hold their teams accountable in the same way.

Step 3: hold leaders within the church accountable for tithing. You probably have numerous leaders within your church who are not paid staff: deacons, elders, and small-group team leaders, for example. As we touched on in part 3, people need to go deeper in their giving commitment as they climb the ladder of leadership in your church. The covenant plays a critical role here. Make sure your lay leaders understand that they are an important part of your ministry team and, as such, are responsible for the commitments they are making to God, the other leaders, and the church as a whole.

Step 4: challenge attenders and members to bring the full tithe to God. We have talked about the importance of using giving challenges to move people to the next level of giving. At no level is that more important than at the tithing level. I cannot overstate the significance of educating people on the tithe and then issuing a time-bound tithe challenge. While challenges apply to all giving levels—for example, you are encouraging non-givers to give for the first time and first-time givers to give regularly—always highlight the challenge's importance specifically for those who need to begin tithing, which, in reality, is everyone who has not yet reached that place on the continuum. The other stops are just stepping stones over which many will be willing to skip.

Tithe Challenge

Let me tell you about the first true tithe challenge we put forth at The Journey. During the second message of a four-part series on stewardship, we decided to hit hard on the importance of bringing the full tithe to God. Our executive pastor started the message by talking about the history of the tithe and how God deserves our best rather than our leftovers. Then I came out to do the second part of the message and explain the tithe challenge. I barely even mentioned giving for the first time or regular giving. Instead, I just shot right to the heart of the issue and let everyone know they should be tithing.

My goal was to challenge everyone in the congregation to commit to tithing for four months. This message was in September, so I was asking them to give the first 10 percent of their income for September, October, November, and December. I knew that, if they agreed, by the end of the four months the tithe would be a regular part of their lives and God would be showing himself to them in a real way. So I laid out the challenge in no uncertain terms. Some may argue I went over the top. I called on them to be serious about their growth. I called on them to be the people God had created them to be. I did everything but tell them God would strike them dead if they didn't give (only kidding). By the time I finished issuing the challenge, I had set the bar pretty high. I was hoping that at least forty or fifty people would be willing to jump over it. Fifty new tithers would really have been something to celebrate.

At the end of the service, I asked those who were interested in taking the tithe challenge to mark the box on the back of their communication card. They didn't know we were planning to send them a copy of *The Treasure Principle* by Randy Alcorn as part of our follow-up with them. I had fifty copies of the book set aside, hoping for that many takers. Are you ready for this? By the end of that day's services, over three hundred people had committed to the tithe challenge. I was eager to lead fifty people into God's plan for stewardship, but as usual his vision was bigger than mine. The next Sunday, I talked about the challenge again, thanked those who had signed up, and gave people another opportunity to jump on board. Another one hundred people took the challenge. All in all, just over four hundred people committed to the four-month tithe challenge.

Did that many people take the challenge because of my eloquence and brilliant articulation? Absolutely not. All I did was try my best to convey what the Bible says about tithing and make those truths relevant to people's lives. Those four hundred people had never been taught to bring the full tithe. In their entire Christian experience, no pastor had ever plainly told them that God made 10 percent the threshold of giving and that Jesus calls us to give at least that much. No one had ever told them that God actually said, "Test me in this." These congregants had been going about their business, trying to grow spiritually, trying to mature, getting connected in small groups, serving when they could, doing all they knew how to do to go deeper in their Christian experience. But we, until that point, had failed to tell them what stewardship means to their discipleship. We had never challenged them to give the full tithe.

The same is true in your church. The Spirit is working in your people. They are trying to mature. They are practicing the spiritual disciplines they know to practice. But they are missing a key component of growth and discipleship because you have been hesitant to lay out the truth about the tithe. Let me encourage you to challenge your people continually in their giving, as we've discussed throughout this book. But every once in a while—maybe once per year—really challenge them to begin tithing, no matter what their current level of giving. How can they hear unless somebody tells them? That's what the tithe challenge is all about—stepping out of your comfort zone and challenging people to step out of theirs.

When you issue a tithe challenge, make sure you follow up right away with the people who accept it. Here's how the process looks:

Sunday: challengers mark the box on their communication card and drop it in the offering bucket.

Monday: your staff compiles a list of those names and enters them into your system.

Wednesday: mail a letter to every person/couple who accepted the challenge, encouraging them to start giving (see fig. 17). We always include a small gift with this letter. A book like *The Generosity Ladder* (Baker, 2010) is perfect. We also include an offering envelope and an auto-debit enrollment form.

Three to four weeks later, send those who accepted the challenge an email (see fig. 18) that includes this two-point message: (1) stay strong in your giving, and (2) realize you are going to be tested. I usually encourage them to read what James has to say about testing and let them know I am available if they need anything.

Jon walks out to the deck with the newspaper and his Bible under one arm and a mug of coffee in the opposite hand. For a minute, he just stands there staring at the leaves—red, gold, and copper—floating down from the tree limbs. He reminds himself to track down the rake later that afternoon.

Jon walks over to the small table on the center of the deck and lowers himself into his favorite chair. Laying his Bible to the side, he opens up the newspaper. The business section tells him that stocks are down again. But at least things at the bank are feeling a little more secure these days. Some

FIGURE 17

September 20—

Dear [first name],

Thank you for accepting the four-month tithe challenge on Sunday. I am excited about your decision to honor God fully with your finances. I can't wait to hear your stories of how God will "open the floodgates of heaven and pour out so much blessing that you will not have room enough for it" (Mal. 3:10).

To assist you in completing the challenge, let me encourage you to do several things:

1. Use an offering envelope every time you give (this way you will be able to track your total giving via the quarterly giving statements).

2. Examine the enclosed sheet on how to automate your giving. Our staff uses this option to ensure that we never miss an opportunity to bring our tithe to God.

3. Take a few minutes over the next four months to read the enclosed book, *The Generosity Ladder*. I trust this book will be a great encouragement to you and help you understand the privilege of giving.

Please know my prayers are with you during this four-month period. From time to time, I will send email encouragements to you and the others in our church who accepted this challenge. Know that Kelley and I are committed to returning our tithe to God and also stretching ourselves to give even more during this same time period.

"But just as you excel in everything—in faith, in speech, in knowledge, in complete earnestness and in your love for us—see that you also excel in this grace of giving" (2 Cor. 8:7).

Sincerely,

Nelson Searcy

Lead Pastor, The Journey Church

Enclosures

For a downloadable version, go to www.MaximizeBook.com.

FIGURE 18

To: Tithe Challenge Participants

From: Nelson Searcy

Subject: Tithe Challenge Check-in

Hello [first name],

It's been a few weeks since you received my letter regarding the four-month tithe challenge. I'm writing this follow-up for two reasons:

1. *To check in and see how the challenge is going.*

I'd love to hear how God is working in you and what God is teaching you. I've heard from several people already, and it's clear that God is blessing those who have accepted this challenge!

2. *To encourage you to stay strong.*

Whenever you make a big commitment to God, it is sometimes followed by a time of testing. It's as if the devil or the world is not happy about our commitment, and it can appear that circumstances are conspiring against us.

While it may not feel like it, God often allows this period of testing not so we will fail but so our faith will go to the next level. Here's a verse to encourage you:

"God blesses those who patiently endure testing and temptation. Afterward they will receive the crown of life that God has promised to those who love him" (James 1:12 NLT).

Thanks for taking the tithe challenge and for honoring God with your finances. I'll check back in a few weeks. In the meantime, I'd love to hear your stories, so feel free to reply to this email.

See you Sunday!

Nelson

P.S. The best way to stay faithful to this challenge is to automate your giving. You can do so through auto-debit giving or through online giving. You can find information about both at www.journeymetro.com/giving.

For a downloadable version, visit www.MaximizeBook.com.

say the economy is on the mend. He's not so sure, but one thing is certain—he hasn't been as worried about money lately. Weird. Things haven't been easy, but then again, they never are.

Frustrated with the negative news, Jon tosses the paper onto the chair beside him and picks up his Bible. He remembers the email he got from Pastor Tim yesterday and flips through the pages until he finds James 1:2–4. "Dear brothers and sisters, when troubles come your way, consider it an opportunity for great joy. For you know that when your faith is tested, your endurance has a chance to grow. So let it grow, for when your endurance is fully developed, you will be perfect and complete, needing nothing" (NLT). Jon reads the words over and over again.

"Maybe James is right," Jon thinks to himself. It has been almost a month since he and Liz took the tithe challenge. Before that, they had been part of another challenge where they started giving regularly. But they weren't giving much, and they knew that something wasn't quite right. When Pastor Tim laid out all the information about the tithe, Jon and Liz both knew that tithing was their next step. And yeah, it had been a little bit of a test during this first month. But things seemed to be going well with the 90 percent they were living on—maybe even better than when they had been living on 100 percent. Was that realization the growth James was talking about?

Jon lays the Bible on his lap and closes his eyes. He hears the breeze rustling in the trees. He hears Madison tapping at the piano in the living room. "All I want, God," Jon whispers, "is for my family to be under your blessing."

He pauses, still a little uncomfortable talking so frankly with God. Then he goes on to say, "Thank you for everything you've given me. The least I can do is give some back to you. Thank you for helping me with that."

Jon opens his eyes when he hears Liz step onto the deck. She plops down next to him and opens up *The Generosity Ladder*.

"Have you looked at this yet?" she asks Jon. "It's pretty good!"

Let me end this section with a note of encouragement. Don't ever feel shy about calling people to the things God has called them to. You didn't create tithing; God did. You are simply the messenger he has sent into your church to educate people. Gordon MacDonald once wrote, "Generous giving is not about doling out extra amounts of money. It is about reorienting the human heart in the direction of Christ so that we become transmitters of the same affection and care that Christ modeled in his time."[13]

As a church leader, you are a model of that affection and care, just as Christ was. Love your people enough to lead them into biblical stewardship. Don't let an underdeveloped theology, fear, or lies of the enemy cause you to become a roadblock to their discipleship. You are the leader. You are accountable to God for giving your people every tool they need to become fully developing followers of Jesus. Biblical stewardship—or bringing the full tithe—is one of those tools. Without it, your people will limp, rather than sprint, through the rest of their spiritual journey.

As a green church planter, there was a time in the not-so-distant past when I was leery of talking about money too much for fear of "offending" someone. In a coaching network with Nelson, I was challenged to wrestle with and clarify for myself what the Bible really has to say about money and then to teach it just as boldly as any other topic. Then a year into our brand-new church, five mature Christian families in our church (aka: our only tithers) moved out of the area within a two-month period. With the backbone of our Maximize system freshly in place (giving envelopes, multiple ways to give, thank-you notes for first-time givers, etc.), I decided to lay out a four-month tithe challenge. To my surprise 75 percent of our families signed up. Now a year and a half later, they're still tithing and we're still growing!

Tommy Duke, Lead Pastor
Iron City Church, Pittsburgh, Pennsylvania
Coaching Network Alumnus

extravagant givers

Spurring People to Live like Jesus

12

extravagant giving

Learning to Live like Jesus

Giving is more than a responsibility—it is a privilege; more than an act of obedience—it is evidence of our faith.

William Arthur Ward

I am praying that you will put into action the generosity that comes from your faith as you understand and experience all the good things we have in Christ.

Philemon 1:6 NLT

What's the first thing you think of when you hear the term *extravagant giver*? If you automatically picture the wealthiest person in your church—the one who gives those sporadic, huge gifts—then you are looking at extravagant giving through the wrong lens. Understanding the truth of extravagant giving involves a bit of a paradigm shift. Here's the reality: anyone in your church can be an extravagant giver, regardless of their wealth or lack thereof. In fact, your church is filled with potential extravagant givers.

"But, Nelson," you may be saying, "you obviously don't know the people in my church. There's really not anyone—not more than one or two, anyway—who can afford to give extravagant gifts." I beg to differ. That assertion is based on a skewed perspective of what extravagant giving really is. In truth, everyone in your church can afford to give extravagant gifts. An extravagant gift is not defined by its amount but by its proportion to the giver's income. Or to put it another way, true generosity is not evidenced in how much a giver gives but in how much she has left.

Remember the old widowed woman who brought her gift to the temple on the day Jesus sat watching the offerings being given? The one he used as an example for everyone within earshot? Do you think any of the religious leaders who saw her hobble up the steps to the temple courts that day in her ragged clothing thought, "Hey, she looks like an extravagant giver! Maybe we should hold her up as an example!" Of course not. I'm sure they all dismissed her ability to give extravagantly based on her obvious low income. Besides, they were already busy schmoozing with the rich people who had come to give an offering. As usual, though, Jesus shined the light of truth on the situation. Luke tells us the story this way: "While Jesus was in the Temple, he watched the rich people dropping their gifts in the collection box. Then a poor widow came by and dropped in two small coins. 'I tell you the truth,' Jesus said, 'this poor widow has given more than all the rest of them. For they have given a tiny part of their surplus, but she, poor as she is, has given everything she has'" (21:1–4 NLT). She was an extravagant giver.

A Life of Generosity

Extravagant giving is the fourth and final step on the stewardship continuum. So far, we've learned how to cultivate first-time gifts, turn first-time givers into regular givers, and move people to obedience by teaching them to tithe. Extravagant giving is the last phase of stewardship development. The tricky part is that it's an extremely fluid stage. Let me explain.

Look again at the stewardship continuum (fig. 19). As we've discussed, the entire continuum has built-in flexibility. Unlike the assimilation system, which moves people through defined stages—first-time guest, second-time guest, regular attender, and member (see *Fusion: Turning First-Time Guests into Fully-Engaged Members of Your Church*, Regal, 2008)—the stewardship system allows for step skipping and backward sliding. While a member can never go back and become a second-time guest again, an extravagant giver can slip back into regular giving. A first-time guest can't become a member on his first visit, but a non-giver can catapult straight to extravagant giving with one gift. The continuum is dynamic.

As I've mentioned several times, the best scenario is to move people to tithing right away. Some brand-new givers will understand the call to tithe and be willing to skip the step of

Figure 19

Stewardship Continuum

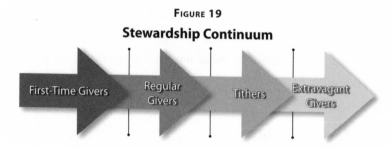

regular giving. This is especially true with new believers and was the case in my own life.

I gave my life to Christ at the age of eighteen, while reading Billy Graham's book *Peace with God*. I prayed the prayer Dr. Graham included in the book's final pages and called the suggested phone number. A woman on the other end of the line told me to get involved in a Bible-believing church—so I did. One of the first things the pastor of that church told me was that I needed to start reading my Bible, praying, connecting with other believers, and tithing—so I did. I remember thinking, "Wow. God has done so much for me. He has saved me from hell, forgiven me, and given me a home in heaven. And all he wants back is 10 percent of my income. That's a great deal!"

Even though my theology on the subject was a little underdeveloped, something in me immediately understood the call to give the tithe to God. My story is not unusual. New Christians are often eager to jump on board with whatever God calls them to do. They are passionate to begin growing in their new faith. As a result, you can often move them right into obedient giving, which is great for both their own development and your church's work. Due to the nature of stewardship progress, they don't have to stop and rest at the regular giving level.

Also because of the continuum's fluidity, any level of giver can jump right to being an extravagant giver—to give sacrificially over and above the tithe. Someone who has never given before can give a huge gift or two and become, for that period of time, an extravagant giver. But he may very well slip back on the continuum if he doesn't understand the heart of baseline giving. Or you can push your tithers to give extravagantly from time to time, which is not a bad thing, but it's not the point. While these extravagant gifts accomplish the important task of stretching the giver—if only briefly—they are not your goal. Instead, you want to encourage your givers to live a life of generosity marked by consistent, predictable, extravagant giving. Big, sporadic gifts are not what extravagant giving is all about.

The goal of the extravagant giving level is to move people to give sacrificially over and above the tithe on a regular basis.

The goal of the extravagant giving level is to move people to give sacrificially over and above the tithe on a regular basis. Note the language of this goal: "over and above the tithe." We need to be less interested in garnering big gifts from those who aren't even tithing and more interested in cultivating ongoing, sacrificial efforts from those who are. While anyone can give extravagantly, this level of giving is most important for drawing tithers deeper into a life of generosity.

As church leaders, we are often prone to turn our attention to the big donor(s) in the church whose once-a-year gift is bigger than everyone else's yearly giving. While that money is great for the budget, and I certainly haven't shied away from accepting it, it does little to disciple the giver. There is a right time and a right way to cultivate big donor gifts, but for the purposes of stewardship as discipleship, our focus should be on helping those who give consistently. How? Through education.

Educating for Extravagance

At each level along the continuum, we educate people on different, specific stewardship truths. To cultivate first-time gifts, we educate people on the biblical basis for giving. To encourage regular givers, we educate them by giving them the tools, resources, and understanding necessary to take that step. To turn regular givers into tithers, we educate them to bring the full tithe to God as an act of joyful worship. So how do we motivate people to stretch even beyond the tithing level and become extravagant givers? How do we instill in them an understanding of biblical generosity? We teach them that the tithe is the minimum.

To move people to give sacrificially over and above the tithe on a regular basis, we teach them that the tithe is merely the jumping-off point for a life of generous giving. As you know by now, each level of stewardship builds on the system's foundation. So as with the other steps along the continuum, we educate people through teaching, challenges, and testimonies.

Teaching

Stewardship teaching is like a canopy that covers all levels of development along the continuum. While people may be standing in different areas under the canopy, its covering is applicable to all of them. For example, when you teach that stewardship is discipleship, everyone benefits, no matter where they are in their journey. Likewise, when you teach people to grow in the grace of giving, the message resonates on every level. Still, it will register with some more than others. As we know, God's Word is alive and active (Heb. 4:12). As such, the importance of growing in the grace of giving will ring especially true with those who are trying to bridge the gap between tithing and extravagant giving.

In the same way, all of your people, no matter what their current level of giving, need to understand that the tithe is the minimum—the base-level amount to be brought back to God—and an offering is anything over and above the tithe. But this teaching will specifically affect those who are ready to go deeper by moving beyond just the tithe into the realm of offerings. Part of this teaching is that the tithe belongs to the local church. There is some freedom in where an offering is given, but by and large I believe it should go back to the local church as well. If your people see your church making a real difference for Jesus, they'll want to give you their full offerings. As your people begin to move toward extravagant giving, encourage them to stretch themselves by giving sacrificially over and above the tithe.

Challenges

Giving challenges look a little different for extravagant givers. While we can throw down the time-bound challenge gauntlet for regular giving and tithing, this model does not work as well for people who are moving toward extravagant giving. The best way to challenge these givers is through infrequent, larger-scale giving opportunities, such as an end-of-year Christmas offering.

We do a Christmas offering every year at The Journey. In a nutshell, it looks like this: we define one primary cause and two or three smaller causes for which we'd like to raise money—usually the big one is missions or evangelism. Then we set a goal for how much we'd like to raise, and schedule and promote the offering. We kick off the offering the weekend before Thanksgiving and run it through the end of the year. In general, we raise about three times our regular weekly offering during this period. More importantly, people are stretched and blessed through the extravagant giving. The Christmas offering has become part of our culture; people know to expect it. Many of our regular attenders and members handle their finances throughout the year with an eye to what they'd like to give to the Christmas offering in December. The regularity of the offering normalizes it and, in turn, encourages people to be consistent in their regular giving. If you aren't currently doing a Christmas offering, you are missing an opportunity to help both your people and your outreach grow. (To learn more about the details of a Christmas offering, see the e-book "How to Plan and Conduct a Christmas Offering" at www. MaximizeBook.com.)

We also use a postmembership class called Class 301 to challenge people to move toward a life of generosity—not just in their giving but in all areas of their lives. We use this class to teach these growing members about extravagant living, answer their questions, and continue discipling them on a deeper level. We teach them how to invest their time, talent, treasure, and testimony. As part of the class, we help people set goals for their giving. When you help people set a goal to stretch themselves to a new plateau of giving and have them put that goal in writing, you are setting a powerful process in motion. Maybe they won't hit the goal, but they will grow in their giving. And they will set a new goal the next year. Setting goals for giving is an incredible tool for creating strong disciples. Figure 20 shows some of the teaching points we cover in Class 301 and our giving worksheet.

Testimonies

My friend and early mentor, Rick Warren, has the best stewardship testimony I've ever heard. It's so powerful, even secondhand, that I share it often. You probably know the story. Rick wrote *The Purpose Driven Life*, which has become the best-selling book of all time next to the Bible. Obviously, that distinction brings with it quite a bit of money. Rick and his wife, Kay, made a decision early on in the book's success that they would become reverse tithers. They live on 10 percent of their income and give 90 percent back to God for kingdom use. So I often tell Rick and Kay's story and say, "You may not be able to be a reverse tither, but maybe you could whittle away at that 90 percent. What is God calling you to? Could you live on 80 percent and give 20 percent?" Testimonies of people who test God and receive his incredible blessing open people's minds and hearts.

Here's the part of Rick's testimony that doesn't get told as often, but it is absolutely vital to the story. As Rick tells it,

FIGURE 20

My Treasure

What I do with my money has implications for . . .

• my relationship with God

The purpose of tithing is to teach you to always put God in first place in your life (Deut. 14:23).

I've never met a spiritually mature Christian who was not mature in giving.

• my church

Did you know?

Currently less than 15 percent of Journey members tithe.

Currently less than 3 percent of Journey attenders tithe.

Currently the average Journey attender gives $ _____ annually.

• eternity

"Don't store up treasures here on earth, where they can be eaten by moths and get rusty, and where thieves break in and steal. Store your treasures in heaven, where they will never become moth-eaten or rusty and where they will be safe from thieves. Wherever your treasure is, there your heart and thoughts will also be" (Matt. 6:19–21 NLT).

Four Ways Spiritual Leaders Invest Their Treasure

1. Give a full 10 percent.

   "A tenth of the produce of the land, whether grain or fruit, belongs to the Lord and must be set apart as holy" (Lev. 27:30 NLT).

   "You should tithe, yes, and you shouldn't leave the more important things undone either" (Matt. 23:23 NLT).

2. Give extravagantly.

   Jesus receives and praises an extravagant gift (Matt. 26:6–13).

   "I assure you, wherever the Good News is preached throughout the world, this woman's deed will be talked about in her memory" (Matt. 26:13 NLT).

3. Give sacrificially.

"He will give you all you need from day to day if you live for him and make the Kingdom of God your primary concern" (Matt. 6:33 NLT).

"They gave as much as they were able, and even beyond their ability. Entirely on their own, they urgently pleaded with us for the privilege of sharing in this service" (2 Cor. 8:3–4).

4. Give cheerfully.

"I want you to excel also in this gracious act of giving. I am not commanding you to do this. But I am testing how genuine your love is by comparing it with the eagerness of the other churches" (2 Cor. 8:7–8 NLT).

"Each one should give what he has decided in his heart to give, not reluctantly or under compulsion" (2 Cor. 9:7).

"Two items clearly reveal the truth about what matters most to us: our checkbooks and our calendars" (Rick Rusaw).

Giving Worksheet

How much do I make in a year (before taxes)? $ _____

My yearly tithe should be (10 percent): $ _____

How much do I make in a month (before taxes)? $ _____

My monthly tithe should be (10 percent): $ _____

How much will I commit to give sacrificially/extravagantly this year:

_____ percent above my regular tithes and offerings.

or

$ _____ above my regular tithes and offerings.

For a downloadable version, see www.MaximizeBook.com.

he and Kay made a decision when they got married that they would faithfully honor God with the tithe and stretch themselves by 1 percent in their giving each year. So the first year of their marriage, they tithed 10 percent. The second year, they tithed 11 percent. The third year, 12 percent, and so on. At the time, Rick was a struggling, young pastor. He didn't have much money. The increase was always a step of faith. But through all those years, Rick was, unknowingly, proving to God that he could be trusted with his worldly wealth. He was proving that his heart was not tied to his money but to the work of the kingdom. And then God chose him to write *The Purpose Driven Life*. I've heard Rick say, "I'm not surprised that God wanted the message of this book to get out there; I'm just surprised he chose me to write it." God chose him because he had shown he could be trusted with the inevitable, impending success. He had proven himself to be a faithful, generous giver.

Even a secondhand testimony, when as powerful as Rick's, can go a long way. Many of your givers will be challenged and inspired by hearing about someone who has been able to live their life at such an extravagant level. Still, make sure you include testimonies in your services from people in your congregation whom other attendees may be able to relate to on a more personal level. Let them see how God is working right now in the life of someone who calls their church home. God loves to speak through his people, so ask his people to speak.

You can also use your own personal testimony. Let me be the first to say that I am often imperfect at holding up the standard of extravagant giving, but Kelley and I are always pushing ourselves to live at this level. I understand the fear that accompanies God's call for you to stretch even more, go even deeper, give more than you've ever given, or give more than you expected to give. But here are two important truths I have learned over the years—two truths I often share with my congregation: first, you can't outgive God. That phrase has almost become a cliché. But clichés usually become clichés for a reason—because they are rooted in truth. You really can't outgive God. Second, obedience leads to certain blessings, both tangible and intangible. When we are eager to stretch ourselves by honoring God through consistent, extravagant giving, he is faithful to keep his promise to throw open the floodgates in our favor. As this truth becomes a reality in your own life, don't hesitate to share it with your people.

Extravagant Follow-up

Many church leaders struggle with the issue of extravagant giver follow-up. They are afraid if they put time and energy into saying thank you to big givers, it will look like they are pandering to them. The key is to strike a balance. Of course you should follow up with your extravagant givers—and that follow-up may look slightly different from the follow-up with regular givers and tithers—but you shouldn't spend an inordinate amount of time and energy doing so. These givers need to be discipled just as much, if not more than, givers at other levels. Don't neglect them, but don't go overboard. Follow up with extravagant givers by acknowledging them, motivating them, encouraging them, and investing in their spiritual growth through various opportunities.

As with other levels of follow-up, simply choose a number that defines the extravagant giving category in your church. At The Journey, this is anyone who gives over $7,000 in a year. Your number may be higher or lower, but really it's arbitrary. When someone breaks through that level consistently—not because of one unusually large gift—move them into the extravagant giver category. As at every level, thank them for their generosity to your church, encourage them, and continue to invest in their spiritual growth through a brief note or thank-you gift. You can also set up times to meet with them one-on-one to thank them for their commitment, just as you would with someone who brings many guests to church or someone who leads a particularly effective small group.

Steve Stroope, another mentor and friend of mine, has a great system for following up with significant givers. On Wednesday of every week, he has breakfast or lunch with a significant giver in his church. Steve's church is over twelve thousand strong, so he may or may not know the givers already. Regardless, he wants to meet these generous people and invest some time in them. Steve meets with a giver and his or her spouse over a casual meal and spends time getting to know them. During the course of the meeting, Steve asks the giver three questions:

1. How can we better minister to you?
2. Is there anything about our church I can clarify for you?
3. How can I pray for you?

These questions provide the giver with a platform to express any concerns or ask questions. Steve understands that unanswered questions can turn into stumbling blocks for some people—stumbling blocks that could trip them up in their extravagant giving. Taking this time to personally acknowledge, motivate, encourage, and invest in extravagant givers is a great idea and well worth the effort. If you have so many extravagant givers in your church that it would be unrealistic to take them all out for a meal, you may need to set the benchmark higher.

On a personal note, I often use everyday meetings and interactions with people in the church to follow up briefly and challenge them to step up their giving. These aren't planned stewardship conversations but just opportunities that present themselves as I go about the work of being a pastor. Basically, I have challenged myself to challenge my people. In other words, I have challenged myself to take advantage of every opportunity God gives me to connect with people and call them to greater generosity. Remember, stewardship is discipleship. Personal discipleship is a gift you can give back to an extravagant giver—and a tool you can use to encourage givers at all levels.

At its core, extravagant giving is about learning to live a life of generosity. I like to think of this final level of giving as the lifestyle level. Once you have helped givers take the step of extravagance—once they are giving sacrificially over and above the tithe on a regular basis—you have discipled them into a deep understanding of God's truth on money and possessions. You have led them to the place where they ought to live out the rest of their lives. No matter how much or how little they have, they understand God is the owner of it all. They have a burden of love to return it to his house for his work. And, most of all, they understand that by grace they are privileged to participate fully in God's plans for his people and his blessings in the church as they live openhanded lives of generosity.

13

getting started

First Steps toward Becoming a Fully Resourced Church

If Christ is not Lord over our money and possessions, then he is not our Lord.

Randy Alcorn

Teach those who are rich in this world not to be proud and not to trust in their money, which is so unreliable. Their trust should be in God, who richly gives us all we need for our enjoyment. Tell them to use their money to do good. They should be rich in good works and generous to those in need, always being ready to share with others. By doing this they will be storing up their treasure as a good foundation for the future so that they may experience true life.

1 Timothy 6:17–19 NLT

Imagine you are sitting in your office. You hear a rapping on the door and look up to see one of your staff members.

"Hey," you say. "What's going on?"

"I just wanted to talk to you about something. I've had this idea on my mind for a few months now. I really feel like God is leading us to make some changes to the volunteer ministry. We need to be doing more to encourage people to get involved. So I've been thinking that if we could spend a little money on . . ."

How do you feel at this moment? Hopefully, thanks to what you've discovered in these pages, your first thought is, "Does God want us to do this?" not, "Can we afford this?" If you can see yourself leaping over the divide between these two dichotomous options—finally able to live consistently in a place of availability and blessing—then this journey we've been on together can be declared a success.

The Dream

My dream for your church and mine is that we would be fully resourced ministries intent on pursuing the dreams and goals God puts before us, that we would never have to say no to an opportunity that might help people grow and advance God's kingdom because of dollars and cents. As you implement the tools and truths of the Maximize system, you will begin to be able to operate your church at full throttle, passionately pursuing God's complete vision for his work on this earth.

Get ready. As you put this system to work, you will see extraordinary things happen in your church. You may see your current number of tithers triple. You may see what is now your yearly budget become your monthly budget. Can you imagine? What could you do for missions, evangelism, ministry, and growth with that kind of money? Start sketching out those possibilities. You may be called on to turn them into reality sooner than you think. God wants his people's money to be used for his purposes. If you are cooperating with him in bringing his plan for stewardship to fruition, he will bless your efforts and trust you with the return.

Some of you may feel overwhelmed. Maybe you are so far from being fully resourced that you don't know if you'll ever get there. You're more concerned with keeping the water running and the front doors open. Perhaps you are struggling with some unrelated issues in your church. As badly as you want to implement the Maximize system, you just aren't sure you can give it the time it deserves right now. To you I say, first of all, you have taken a huge step by reading this book. You've begun your education and opened yourself up to some important realities. Second, don't be discouraged. I challenge you to start where you are. Remember, this system begins with you and works its way down to your members. So if you can't do anything else, look inward. Begin by developing your own unshakable stewardship theology. Continue to study what the Bible has to say about giving and decide to honor those principles in your own life. To that end, let me encourage you to make four personal stewardship commitments that will help you grow as a giver and prepare you to lead your church into a deeper level of discipleship:

1. Commit your financial life to God.
2. Begin giving your regular tithe and stretch yourself toward extravagant giving.
3. Take the necessary steps to live debt-free for the rest of your life.
4. Continue your stewardship education.

Once you get your own financial life on track, you will be able to implement the Maximize system with much more integrity and enthusiasm.

Big Rocks

While you are in that process—or if you already have your own financial stewardship under control—decide to put a few key components of the overall system in place. These components will breathe life into your church's giving no matter what its current state and will begin to shift the underlying momentum toward generosity. Then when you are ready to implement the system fully, you will already have these "big rocks" set.

You've probably heard about the professor who walked into his classroom one day with an empty jar. In fact, if you've read my book *Ignite: How to Spark Immediate Growth in Your Church* (Baker, 2009), I know you've heard it, because I tell the story there. It bears repeating and examining from a slightly different angle.

One day, a wise professor set out to prove a point to a bunch of sleepy students. He walked into his classroom with a big, widemouthed jar under his arm. He made his way to the front of the room and set the jar on his desk. With the students paying little attention, he filled the jar with five big stones. He put the stones in one by one until the jar couldn't hold anymore. Then he asked his students, "Is this jar full?" They half nodded their assertion that it was.

The professor pulled a bucket of pebbles from under his desk. Slowly, he poured the pebbles into the jar. They bounced and settled into the small spaces between the stones. Once again, the professor asked his students, who were now slightly more awake, "Is this jar full?" They all quietly contended that, yes, of course it was.

The professor proceeded to pull another bucket from beneath his desk—this one filled with fine sand. As the students looked on, he poured the sand into the jar. The granules quickly filled in the barely visible cracks and crevices between the stones and pebbles. This time when asked, "Is this jar full?" the class answered with a resounding, "Yes!"

In response to his students' certainty, the professor reached under his desk and brought out a pitcher of water. The students watched in amazement as the professor poured the entire pitcher into the jar.

Then the professor asked a different question. "What was the point of this demonstration? What was I trying to teach you through this now-full jar?"

A student in the back called out, "You were showing us that you can always fit more things into your life if you really work at it."

"No," replied the professor. "The point is that you have to put the big rocks in first or you'll never get them in."

Back to the five big rocks of the Maximize system. If you can't do everything suggested in these pages right away, put the five big rocks in place. Without them, nothing else we've discussed will be effective, and with them, you will be light-years ahead of where you are now. Once you put the five big rocks in place, you can work on filling the space between them at your own pace. The five big rocks are:

1. Model biblical stewardship in your own life (see chap. 11).
2. Send a handwritten thank-you note to every first-time giver (see chap. 6).
3. Provide offering envelopes and teach your people to use them (see chap. 5).
4. Reevaluate and streamline your offering procedures (see chap. 5).
5. Mail out quarterly giving statements. If you can't do quarterly statements right away, start with semiannual statements (see chap. 9).

If you put these rocks into the jar of your stewardship system, you will have made huge strides down the path toward maximizing your giving. As you see your people move into deeper realms of stewardship understanding—and as that understanding is reflected in the new money being brought into your church—take the time to celebrate. Keep track of how your stewardship system is growing and thank God for the blessings he is bringing your way as you cooperate with him.

Stewardship as Discipleship

We began this journey together by underscoring the fact that stewardship is discipleship. Let me remind you of that truth one more time as we close. You and I, as leaders of Christ's church, have been called to be shepherds of the people placed in our care. Here's one thing we all know about the souls we've been entrusted with: they are highly focused on, confused about, and concerned with money. Their hearts are weighed down because their only understanding of their treasure is deeply rooted in the thinking of this world. The time has come, fellow church leader, for you and me to step up and shine the light of God's truth on our people's financial lives.

If we internalize the biblical principles we've been studying and decide to be faithful in implementing them, we can spark a revolution in the church. We can live in a reality in which our churches are free to do the work God is calling us to regardless of the cost . . . a reality in which the Great Commission is not only talked about but also acted upon without restraint. We can excel, corporately, in the grace of giving and reap the eternal benefits. Remember Peter's admonition in 1 Peter 5:1–4:

> I appeal to you: Care for the flock that God has entrusted to you. Watch over it willingly, not grudgingly—not for what you will get out of it, but because you are eager to serve God. Don't lord it over the people assigned to your care, but lead them by your own good example. And when the Great Shepherd appears, you will receive a crown of never-ending glory and honor (NLT).

Given Jesus's assertion that "wherever your treasure is, there the desires of your heart will also be" (Matt. 6:21 NLT), I can't think of a more important area where we need to be beyond reproach in caring for our people than in the area of their giving. By dealing openly and honestly with how they view and manage their earthly treasure, we are directing the desires of their hearts back toward the things of God.

If we internalize the biblical principles we've been studying and decide to be faithful in implementing them, we can spark a revolution in the church.

Jesus embraced every chance he had to talk about money. Let's make him as much our example in this aspect of discipleship as we do in any other. Let's loosen the bond that money has on people and usher them to a place of maturity. Let's shine a light on this critical issue, forever destroying the shroud of darkness that has so long encased it. God's work on this earth begins with you and me—and with our willingness to call people to a higher standard in every area. As we do that, we will truly give them the best possible opportunity to become fully developing followers of Jesus. But not only that, we will also give them a collective church in which there is unhindered opportunity to participate in the advancement of God's kingdom.

afterword

I hope this book will become a conversation starter between us. I am constantly developing resources and gathering ideas from others to help you lead a fully resourced church. In fact, I recently held a private event for my coaching alumni where I taught everything I know about stewardship (it would fill at least three books like this one) called The Stewardship Intensive. You can find information about securing the recording of this intensive at the following website:

www.MaximizeBook.com

You can also use the website to connect with me. I would love to hear your story and to continue discussing the ways we can grow together for God's glory.

Your partner in ministry,
Nelson Searcy,

Lead Pastor, The Journey Church,
www.JourneyMetro.com

Founder, www.ChurchLeaderInsights.com

notes

1. Empty Tomb, Inc., October 15, 2009, www.emptytomb.org/table1_07. html.

2. Randy Alcorn, *Money, Possessions, and Eternity* (Wheaton: Tyndale, 2003), 8.

3. Andy Stanley, *Fields of Gold* (Wheaton: Tyndale, 2004), 15–16.

4. Ibid., 17.

5. Gary Thomas, *Sacred Marriage* (Grand Rapids: Zondervan, 2000), 154.

6. "Americans Donate Billions to Charity, but Giving to Churches Has Declined," Barna Research Online, April 25, 2005, http://barna.org, p. 1.

7. Stephen King, www.stephenking.com/news_archive/archive_2001.html.

8. Alcorn, *Money, Possessions, and Eternity*, 13.

9. Alcorn, *Money, Possessions, and Eternity*, 182.

10. Ibid.

11. Howard Dayton, *Your Money Counts* (Gainesville, GA: Crown Financial Ministries, 1996), 74.

12. Alcorn, *Money, Possessions, and Eternity*, 186.

13. Gordon MacDonald, *Pursuing Godly Character*, Generous Giving, www.crown.org/LIBRARY/ViewArticle.aspx?ArticleId=174.

Nelson Searcy is the founding lead pastor of The Journey Church of the City with locations in New York City, Queens, Brooklyn, and Boca Raton, FL. He is also the founder of www.ChurchLeaderInsights.com. He and his church appear routinely on lists such as the 50 Most Influential Churches and the 25 Most Innovative Leaders. Searcy lives in New York City.

Jennifer Dykes Henson is a freelance writer based in New York City. She has served as a writer/producer and ministry consultant to organizations across the East Coast. Prior to moving to New York, Jennifer worked with Dr. Charles Stanley as the manager of marketing communications for In Touch Ministries in Atlanta, Georgia.

STEP-BY-STEP PLAN TO FINANCIAL EXCELLENCE

The Generosity
Ladder

by Nelson Searcy

9780801072765

112 pp. • $6.99p

The Generosity Ladder is the quintessential guidebook for anyone who desires to handle money with excellence. Written as an answer to all of the questions and misunderstandings that surround the intersection of God and money, *The Generosity Ladder* clarifies, once and for all, what the Bible really says about honoring God with our finances and details a step-by-step plan for attaining financial excellence.

Published alongside *Maximize*, Nelson Searcy's much-anticipated stewardship guidebook for church leaders, *The Generosity Ladder* will allow laypeople to fully grasp God's plan for their finances, acknowledge their current level of stewardship, and chart out the steps they need to take in order to handle money in a way that honors God.

BakerBooks
a division of Baker Publishing Group
www.BakerBooks.com